THE
IRREVOCABLE
CALLING

ISRAEL'S ROLE AS A LIGHT TO THE NATIONS

DANIEL C. JUSTER, TH.D.

Lederer Books
a division of
Messianic Jewish Publishers
Clarksville, Maryland

All Scripture quotations, unless otherwise indicated, are taken from the *Complete Jewish Bible* © 1998 by David H. Stern, published by Jewish New Testament Publications, Inc.

Cover Design by
Josh Huhn, Design Point, Inc.

2015   3

ISBN 13: 978-1-880226-34-6
ISBN 10: 1-880226-34-0

Library of Congress Control Number: 2007925411
Printed in the United States of America

Lederer Books
a division of
Messianic Jewish Publishers
P.O. Box 615
Clarksville, MD 21029

Distributed by
Messianic Jewish Resources International
Order line: (800) 410-7367
E-mail: lederer@messianicjewish.net
Website: www.messianicjewish.net

This book is dedicated to my first born son,
Benjamin W.D. Juster.
Ben has been a great joy and support to us,
for he carries on the values and vision that are so very dear to us.
His handling our affairs on the American side of the Ocean
makes it possible for us to live in Israel.
He and his wife, Lorena,
have given us wonderful grandchildren.
May he see great fruitfulness in his life.

Other books by author

Jewish Roots
A Foundation of Biblical Theology

That They May Be One
*A Brief Review of Church Restoration Movements
and Their Connection to the Jewish People*

Passion for Israel
*A Short History of the Evangelical Church's
Commitment to the Jewish People and Israel*

Conveying A Heritage
A Messianic Jewish Guide to Home Practice

Mutual Blessing
Discovering the Ultimate Destiny of Creation

Jewishness and Jesus

Relational Leadership
*A Manual of Leadership Principles for
Congregational Leaders and Members*

Growing to Maturity
A Messianic Jewish Guide

Dynamics of Spiritual Deception

The Biblical World View
An Apologetic

Due Process
A Plea for Biblical Justice Among God's People

Israel, the Church and the Last Days

Revelation
The Passover Key

All books available through
Messianic Jewish Resourses Int'l
800-410-7367
www.messianicjewish.net

CONTENTS

FOREWORD

If you have ever wondered why in recent years so much of the Church has begun to talk about Israel and the Jewish people . . .

If you have thought that Jewish people who come to faith should just join a church like everyone else . . .

If you have considered what, if any, the reestablishment of the State of Israel really has to do with prophecy . . . then you need to read this book.

If you would like to delve more deeply into the heart of Paul the Jewish apostle whose life's calling was to the Gentiles . . .

If you want to understand more completely the center section of Paul's letter to the Romans, chapters 9 through 11, that speaks specifically of Israel and the Jewish people and how this relates to future generations . . . then you need to read this book.

Dan Juster is a man of remarkable ability. He is one of the foremost scholars among the resurrected Jewish family of faith in Yeshua/Jesus. He has an extraordinary intellectual ability to perceive truth, but he knows that intellect alone is not enough. Only a "mind controlled by the Spirit" produces life and peace (Romans 8:6). The combination of intellect and spirit has produced in Dan a man that is being used mightily in God to bring Jews and Gentiles together in Messiah.

One of the great joys of my life has been serving with Dan and his fellow covenant *Tikkun* partners. I do not know of any group where integrity is respected more highly. For ten years, I also have traveled the world with Dan and the *Toward Jerusalem Council II* committee as we went on prayer journeys to strategic places where, in earlier years, decrees were made against the Jewish people (Spain, Nicea, Auschwitz), repenting for the sins of the past. We also made diplomatic connections to some of today's top Church leaders from the historic churches to the leaders of charismatic and evangelical denominations.

Dan has a voice that needs to be heard. I pray your own heart will be open to the voice of God as you listen to his comments on *The Irrevocable Calling* of Israel.

Don Finto
Pastor Emeritus, Belmont Church, Nashville, Tennessee
Director, The Caleb Company

CHAPTER ONE

ISRAEL'S ETERNAL CALLING

The ultimate destiny of Israel remains one of the most compelling questions for Christians today. This is partly a response to the modern state of Israel, in existence for almost 60 years, living within her ancient borders according to biblical prophecy. Popular biblical interpretations have also changed, as ministers and academics are less likely to present biblical Israel and the Jewish people as mere illustrations for a future, triumphant Church. Indeed, many evangelical Christians hold a positive view of the Jewish people. But the issues concerning Israel's calling are complex and require openness to new perspectives and insights that still elude many among us.

This era has also seen the rise of a growing international Messianic Jewish movement, as a significant number of Jewish people embrace Yeshua as Messiah and accept the New Covenant Scriptures. Hundreds of Messianic congregations worldwide—including more than 100 throughout Israel—allow Jewish believers to retain the ethnic, cultural and spiritual identities that they feel are enhanced by their new faith. The unprecedented appearance of a global Messianic Jewish community should give Christians more incentive to better understand Israel's call and destiny from a contemporary perspective.

However, the definitive explanation of this question belongs to a Jewish believer from another age. In Romans 9–11, Rabbi Shaul (the Apostle Paul) unconditionally declares that ethnic, national Israel still counts in the plan of God. Her "stumbling" over the issue of Messiah's identity is temporary. Gentile believers in particular are called to encourage Israel to desire the spiritual hope they have found in Yeshua, although the apostle expected that only a part of Israel would be reached by the message (Rom. 11:14).

Paul foresaw that growing numbers of Jewish believers would be an important sign of Messiah's return, providing greater blessings for all believers until the moment when Israel fully turns to Messiah Yeshua, which will be "life from the dead" (Rom. 11:15). This interpretation is common among the best Bible commentators.

Paul concludes by revealing the "mystery" of ethnic-national Israel's future destiny:

1

> .... and that it is in this way that all Isra'el will be saved. As the
> *Tanakh* says, "Out of Tziyon will come the Redeemer; he will
> turn away ungodliness from Ya'akov and this will be my cov-
> enant with them…when I take away their sins." With respect to
> the Good News they are hated for your sake. But with respect to
> being chosen they are loved for the Patriarchs' sake, for God's
> free gifts and his calling are irrevocable. (Rom. 11:26–29)

Although all believers may apply this Scripture to gifts they receive
from Yeshua in the Spirit, these verses, in context, clearly emphasize that
the irrevocable call is the call of Israel.

Primarily, we want to understand the calling of Israel and its full
significance as Paul did. Every generation, from Paul's to our own, has
been discouraged and often overwhelmed by world events that keep us
from trusting the Scriptures. As we explore Israel's history and spiritual
development, we will see how our contemporary situation fits into the
apostle's future vision and that his confidence in Israel's destiny is
rooted in God's enduring, inspirational faithfulness.

Secondly, we need to discern the nature of God's gift and call to Israel today. Some prefer to see Israel's calling as a gift to a future,
Millennial Age; others look back and see the height of Israel's spiritual
legacy in the era of the Mosaic Covenant. But in our time, although the
state of Israel is prominently visible on the world stage, few say anything
on how God is currently at work in the life of the Jewish people and how
he has gifted them to bless the present generation.

It is ironic that Christians have historically ignored the original New
Testament approach to Jewish believers in Yeshua. In contrast with popular opinion, the writers of the New Covenant Scriptures (all of whom were
Jewish, except for Luke) assumed that Yeshua's first followers were acting
in continuity with God's prophetic gifting and call to Israel.

Most important, Paul identifies the first-century Jewish followers of
Yeshua as the saved remnant of ethnic, national Israel (Rom. 11:5). He
repeatedly describes himself as an example of God's continuing faithfulness: an "Israelite of the tribe of Benjamin" (Rom. 11:1) and stresses
that God is working through him. His own salvation and the salvation of
the remnant of Israel are proof that God has not abandoned the nation
as a whole.

The inclusion of Gentiles through the New Covenant does not in-
validate Israel's calling. However, it extends the priesthood and the
meaning of being the people of God to those called from all nations.
Those from the nations are grafted into a Jewish olive tree (Rom. 11:24).

As we will see, there are separate callings for Jews and Gentiles and these have both parallels and differences.

Finally, the importance of the growing international community of Messianic Jews has to be recognized. Many Christians have assumed that by embracing Yeshua, the Jewish believers of the past and present are somehow disconnected from Israel and her calling, either in full or in part. But if, as Paul indicates, Messianic Jews are a sign of the irrevocable call of the Nation of Israel, how do Israel's calling and gifts apply to them? Also, what do their increasing numbers mean for our time?

Apart from Paul's extended analysis in Romans, the New Testament has only limited explanations of the gifts and calling of God to Israel, which has led some to overlook the issue and dismiss the significance of the Messianic Jewish movement. However, for first century believers, the primary source for detailed explanations on Israel's gifts and calling was the Hebrew Scriptures.

We will begin to seek a foundational understanding of Israel's irrevocable calling (past, present and future) by studying the doctrine of Israel according to the Hebrew Bible. Then we will ask how the New Covenant Scriptures provide further insights on the issue of Israel's eternal destiny.

CHAPTER TWO

THE CALLING OF ISRAEL FROM ABRAHAM TO MOSES

The Bible does not begin with Genesis 12. Why? Because Genesis 1–11 provides the setting for us to comprehend God's purpose in choosing Abraham. The call of Abraham in chapter 12 reflects God's heart of redemption for a world that has fallen under bondage, as described in chapters 1–11. God's purpose is to redeem the whole world.

Genesis 1-11 describes the fall of Adam and Eve into sin, the first blood sacrifice, the promise of redemption to come through the seed of the woman (Gen. 3:15), the flood, and the scattering of the human race over the face of the earth. The separation of people and languages are explained as well. Universal history precedes the story of Israel, for God is the Lord of all the earth.

The bridge between universal history and the history of Israel is the call of Abraham described in Genesis 12:1–3. Abraham is promised that his seed would bring blessing to all the nations of the earth. "And by you all the families of the earth will be blessed." (Gen. 12:3). This is God's purpose, to make Abraham an instrument of God for the redemption of the whole world.

The life of Abraham is foundational to understanding the gift and call of God to his descendents, the Nation of Israel. Before God's call came to Abraham, he held lineage in a chosen line from Shem. Abraham's father was traveling to the Promised Land, but stopped and settled in Haran. Although the family compromised with paganism, the light of God was not extinguished; there was a difference between Abraham's family and the rest of the world. Abraham's son, Isaac, and later his grandson, Jacob, were encouraged to find wives from their relatives in Haran.

Abraham was set apart by an ability to hear the voice of the Creator. He obeyed and not only became the physical father of God's sanctified people, Israel, but also the spiritual father of all those who are sanctified by a life of faithfulness and obedience to God. Were others called before Abraham? Did they refuse? Were they in too much darkness to hear the call? We are not told.

Abraham is directed to leave his family and go to the Land that God will show him. God promises that he will become a great nation and gives him the land of Canaan. He will bless those who bless Abraham and curse those who curse him. In his seed, all the nations of the world will be blessed. The words of this passage reflect the traditions and culture of a covenant relationship based on strong friendship where friends are shared with friends and one's enemies are also one's friend's enemies. Each party to the covenant is expected to be loyal unto death. Each can require the most prized possession of the other to prove the covenant. We see this last feature in the covenant passages of Genesis 12–22.

The covenant of strong friendship is a blood covenant, either by the parties sharing in their own blood, like Native Americans, or through a substitute sacrificial animal. Today, scholars describe this type of covenant as a "kinship covenant."

In Genesis 15, when the covenant is confirmed, Abraham is told to look at the night sky. His descendants will be as numerous as the stars of the heavens and the sand of the sea. The supernatural presence of God confirms this covenant with an oath marked by the passing of smoke and fire between the pieces of Abraham's sacrificial offering. This is blood covenanting from God's side and in Genesis 17 the covenant is again confirmed. Abraham is given the commandment of circumcision, a further blood covenant sign for his descendants, traditionally cut on the male child's eighth day. The covenant passes from father to son throughout all generations.

As Abraham's physical descendents continue to enter the covenant, they will form a distinctive ethnic, national people. In particular, they are identified by their connection to a specific location, a piece of real estate from which they will live out this calling. The promise of this specific land to Abraham's descendants, the land of Canaan, is repeated in each passage that reaffirms the covenant. Somehow, being a distinct people in this land is part of God's plan for using Abraham's descendants to bring blessing to all the nations of the earth.

The great puzzle is that Abraham and Sarah have no children. How can the covenant promises be fulfilled? Abraham and Sarah take it upon themselves to produce a child from Hagar, Sarah's maidservant, a common practice in ancient times when a wife proved barren. For a time, Abraham believes that Hagar's son, Ishmael, is heir to the promises. However, God again comes to Abraham and makes it clear that a son from Sarah would be his heir. By a great miracle, the elderly Sarah conceives a child. In a rejuvenating miracle, Abraham and Sarah are able to have a child when both are well beyond their child producing years. The child of promise, Isaac, is born.

The Sacrifice of Isaac

I have discussed God's covenant with Abraham to prepare us for a full appreciation of Genesis 22. This chapter is foundational for understanding the gift and call of God to Israel. Here, God calls Abraham to sacrifice his son Isaac as a burnt offering. It is an astonishing passage. Why would God make such a demand? Isaac is described compassionately as Abraham's only son: "Take your son, your only son, whom you love, Yitz'chak" (Gen. 22:2). The sacrifice will take place where God shows him. Abraham is led to Mount Moriah.

Isaac is a youth, perhaps of bar mitzvah age (13). He asks his father, "Where is the lamb for a burnt offering?" Abraham answers, "God will provide" (Gen. 22:7, 8). When they build the altar and lay out the wood for the fire, Isaac lies down on the altar; the text makes no mention of any protest. But as Abraham raises the knife to slay his boy, the Angel of God stops him. Nearby, Abraham sees a ram caught by its horns in a thicket, and the animal is offered instead, a substitution for Isaac. After the episode, which is understood to have been an ultimate test of faith and obedience, God affirms more forcefully than ever before the original terms of the covenant with Abraham (and now Isaac). The Lord restates that the patriarch's seed will bless all the nations of the earth, and Abraham's descendants will inherit the land of Canaan as their perpetual possession.

God's command to Abraham that he sacrifice Isaac tested the limits of his covenant friendship by demanding that the father surrender his most precious possession, the life of his son. Indeed, the life of Isaac was more precious to Abraham than his own life. The entire incident prophetically foreshadows the sacrifice of Messiah Yeshua.

God gave his only Son, a child of miraculous birth, to die for our sins. He is the Son of the promise through whom blessing comes to the whole world. We might say that God is responding in kind to Abraham and has also given that which was most precious to him, the life of his Son to complete the covenant of strong friendship. One might hold the view that the sacrifice of Isaac was necessary and without it, the sacrifice of Yeshua could not have taken place. Clearly, the events are linked. This interpretation corresponds to the widely understood meaning of the covenant of strong friendship.

In addition, there are profound implications for the priesthood of Israel. The sacrifice takes place on Mount Moriah, where Israel's Temple will be built and sacrifices offered for one thousand years. Abraham powerfully demonstrates here that he is the father of the priestly line. As the book of Hebrews says, the priests were in the loins of Abraham and when the patriarch presented offerings to God through King Melchizedek, a priest-king whose titles prefigure Messiah Yeshua, he was actually giving offerings to the higher priesthood of Yeshua (Hebrews 7). Apparently, Abraham on Moriah founds the mantle of priesthood in ancient Israel on the sacrifice of Isaac. An understanding of the essential meanings of this sacrifice provides a foundational understanding of ancient Israel's sacrificial system.

What are the spiritual implications of the sacrifice of Isaac? First, the sacrifice of Isaac is a priestly repudiation of the sin of Adam and Eve and a representative act for the whole human race. When Adam and Eve fell into sin, they were attempting to assert their autonomy from God. The serpent claimed that in knowing good and evil, that is by determining good and evil for themselves through experience, they would become gods. The root of sin is found in this rebellion, self-sufficiency and quest for autonomy, desiring to be gods themselves. Yeshua taught, "Apart from me you can't do a thing" (John 15:5). Adam and Eve made a fateful decision to believe Satan and to act on the premise that they could live apart from their Father-Creator.

The Hebrew Scriptures present a corporate view of humanity. Not only are we individuals before God but, together, form the human race. Our lives are intertwined with one another reaching back to Adam. All of us sinned in Adam according to Romans 5. But when Abraham sacrificed Isaac on the altar, it was a priestly act, a renunciation of the roots of sin in rebellion and autonomy. It was a corporate priestly act in representation for the whole human race. Abraham gave himself wholly to the Father by this act of obedience, though it made no sense in an experiential way. His actions were the deliberate opposite of those committed by Adam and Eve.

Abraham's ultimate act of obedience and submission was the culmination of many smaller acts in obedient response to the call of God. For Abraham, to give up his own life would have been little in comparison to offering his son. Any genuine father would affirm that his ongoing essence is in his child. Preserving the son's life is central to the father's own meaning. Therefore, Abraham offering his son was a greater sign of his submission to God, of giving his all, than any other possible response. In this event, Abraham functioned as the high priest of the whole human race and offered humanity back to God through his own representative act.

Abraham became a high priest of the whole human race. In this function, he became both the physical and spiritual father of the Levitical priests and all of Israel's high priests. In addition, Abraham established the meaning of the sacrificial priesthood by offering Isaac on

Mount Moriah. Isaac was a human sacrifice, yet, he was offered only symbolically since the Angel of the Lord stopped Abraham before he killed his son. This human sacrifice most perfectly points to the Coming One, the Messiah, who lays down his life for our sins. When the Temple was established on Moriah, a connection was made between the sacrifices in relation to their ultimate meaning. All of the sacrifices looked back to the sacrifice of Isaac for their foundational meaning and forward to Yeshua for their ultimate fulfillment.

In addition, every time the priests offered an animal in sacrifice to God, they were performing an act of intercessory representation: they were offering Israel and the nations back to God. Even the individual's offerings for their sins (the sin offering) and the burnt offering which followed were not only for the sake of the individual but participated relationally to the sacrifice of Isaac for they were offered by the Levitical priests on Moriah.

God was pleased with Abraham, who by faith had fully yielded his heart. Abraham's obedience set in motion the spiritual laws that would eventually lead to the salvation of the human race through the work of Yeshua. When Messiah Yeshua laid down his life on the cross, he also gave himself fully to the Father's will. Through faith in his sacrifice, we can offer ourselves to the Father. The power of evil and of the Fall is thwarted. In him, the prodigal returns to the Father's house and affirms that without him we can do nothing (John 15:5).

As we further comprehend the meaning of Israel's call as it was developed in the Mosaic Covenant, these themes will be expanded. However, we can now see that the concept of priesthood is foundational for understanding the call of Israel. The call of Israel is to function for humanity in the essential priestly role before God for the sake of the redemption of the world. This priestly role operated initially through the sacrificial system where intercession was made for the sins of Israel and for the whole human race, that all might come back to God. But its firm foundation would remain the powerful covenant relationship between God and Abraham.

CHAPTER THREE

THE CALLING OF ISRAEL IN THE MOSAIC COVENANT

As the Abrahamic Covenant is foundational for the salvation of the world, the Mosaic Covenant is foundational for the coming of Messiah and the *B'rit Hadashah* (the New Covenant). As we see later, the New Covenant permanently applies and fulfills the principles of the Abrahamic Covenant and Mosaic Covenants (McComiskey).

The biblical texts for the Mosaic Covenant are found in Exodus through Deuteronomy with the key verse found in Exodus 19:6: "You will be a kingdom of *cohanim* for me, a nation set apart." What is the function of this priesthood? The priesthood brings the people to God and God to the people.

Israel's priesthood fulfills its purpose in several dimensions. First, their most significant visible role is in the sacrificial system. Second, during the "designated times" of the Lord they serve to illustrate God's truth. These two functions are linked because the sacrificial dimension is part of the designated times. Third, the priesthood acts as a testimony to the nations by exhibiting Israel's quality of life, a result of its submission to the Torah, the instruction of God. This foreshadows the Kingdom of God. Finally, the priesthood is a witness to the power of God in the midst of Israel and his ultimate place as Lord over all the earth. I refer to the last two dimensions as the witness of national character formed by the Torah and the charisma or power-gifting of God who dwells in the midst of the nation. An obedient people would be invincible because of the invincibility of God.

In order to fully appreciate the biblical concept of priesthood, we need to comprehend the principle of representational righteousness. Because God sees humanity as a whole, the righteousness of a few may stave off judgment for the many. Thus, Abraham could plead for God to deliver the entire city of Sodom on the basis of finding there a small number of good men. Moses and Aaron prayed effectively for God to lessen the penalty of judgment on Israel. To this day, High Holy Day prayers in the synagogue plead for mercy based on the sacrifice of Isaac or for the sake of the righteousness of Israel's spiritual fathers, Abraham, Isaac and Jacob.

The height of representational righteousness is accomplished in Ye-shua, whose individual sacrifice atones for the whole human race. Be-lievers continue to see the benefit of intercessory prayer as the intercessor connects personally and becomes part of the corporate real-ity of those for whom they are in prayer. When God declares that Israel is to be a nation of priests, they are called to live as intercessory represen-tatives before God for the sake of the nations of the world. Israel acts as a corporate nation to represent corporate humanity.

Priestly Representation through the Sacrificial System

While Israel as a whole is a kingdom of priests, the nation itself is orga-nized to fulfill the priestly functions through specific tribal and family vocations. Levites (from the tribe of Levi) are called to act as the priests in Israel. The descendants of Aaron are called to be *Cohanim* (High Priests), standing before God to represent Israel, the Levites, and the na-tions. As well, the whole nation participated in various ways.

The Temple on Mount Moriah in Jerusalem was central to the priesthood. For approximately four hundred years before King Solomon (circa 950 B.C.E.), the sacrifices were offered in a movable tabernacle. But afterwards, and for almost one thousand years, sacrifices were of-fered in a succession of Temple buildings. Shortly before the time of Ye-shua, Herod transformed the physical landscape, raising a massive stone framework to cover Mount Moriah and then built on top of that his massive Temple complex. Although Herod's Temple was destroyed in 70 C.E., the stonework base over the mount remains largely intact. (This in-cludes the famed Western Wall, a site sacred to Israel for its location, closest to the ancient Temple's Holy of Holies. The upper area, formerly the site of the Temple, is now controlled by Muslims and best known for the landmark Dome of the Rock.)

It is amazing to contemplate that for approximately fourteen hun-dred years, blood sacrifices were offered to God before Yeshua came, a sacrificial system for the sake of the whole world. Indeed, Solomon prayed (2 Chron. 6) that when anyone from the nations prayed toward the Temple, he would have his prayers answered and sins forgiven.

Consider the universal implications of this long history of sacrifice for all humanity. Every autumn, five days after the great fast day of Yom Kippur, when the entire Nation of Israel received atonement for their sins, they began to celebrate the feast of Sukkot (Tabernacles). During this eight-day feast, seventy bulls were offered on the altar, seventy being the symbolic number of the nations of the world. This was a specific sign that Israel acted as the priestly representative before God on behalf of all the nations of the world. More than this, because Abraham's offering of his son made him the high priest representative for the whole human race and all Israel's sacrifices are rooted in the sacrifice of Isaac on Moriah, every sacrifice offered in that place had an element of representation on behalf of the nations of the world.

The same principle was at work when individual Israelites brought sacrifices to atone for personal sins. They were also fulfilling Israel's priestly function as they made offerings. Their sacrifices included those for individuals, for families (the Passover sacrifice), for the whole nation (Yom Kippur), and for the nations of the world (Sukkot).

The Basic Blood Sacrifice

Let's take a closer look at the sacrifices. Leviticus 1–3 lays out four basic types of sacrifice that were required of Israel when a person sinned. Each type showed a necessary part of the process to restore one's relationship with God.

The first type of sacrifice is a *sin offering*. This takes away the objective judgment against the sinner for violating the Torah. The second type is the *guilt offering* which assuages the conscience and its guilt, for the animal bears our guilt. The penalty of the law must be satisfied by the death of the transgressor. In these two offerings, we see a substitute for the one who sins. In both, part of the offering is burned on the altar as a sweet smelling aroma before God, and the priest eats the remainder. This symbolizes the dissolution of our sin and guilt in the righteous representative, the priest.

The third type, the *burnt offering*, allows a person to dedicate himself wholly to God, shown through the symbol-picture of the animal being fully consumed by burning on the altar. After the act of dedication, the worshipper can have fellowship with God. This is symbolized in the fourth type, the *fellowship offering* (also called *peace offering*). Part of this offering is burned completely (God's portion in fellowship), the priest eats part, and the worshipper before God with a renewed sense of the divine fellowship eats a part. The same elements are present even in corporate offerings, for example, the Passover sacrifice when the family shares the Passover lamb in fellowship with God.

All of the animal offerings had overlapping meaning as well as distinct emphases. Every one was a blood sacrifice. Each of them had a substitution-atonement dimension. In every kind, the animal died in place of the sinner. The worshipper placed his hands on the head of the animal thereby transferring his guilt and shame. The animal died in their place and the priest consumed the sin and guilt in three of the four types of sacrifice.

The sacrifices represent about fourteen hundred years of blood being shed, reservoirs of blood. Did the sacrifices accomplish anything? Did we need hundreds of years of sacrifices just to symbolize the sacrifice of Yeshua? The book of Hebrews tells us that the blood of bulls and goats can not take away sin. Spilling the blood of another creature can not truly cleanse a conscience. But there is more to it. I believe that all of these sacrifices were intercession for the coming of the Messiah and the salvation of the world. This is the meaning of the sacrifice of Isaac; it is the meaning of all that follows. Our prayers in Yeshua's name cannot save us, but they do connect us to the atonement of Yeshua. In a similar fashion, Israel's sacrifices participated in the meaning of what they foreshadowed, the perfect sacrifice of Yeshua as the effective atonement for sin.

Because Israel's rites of sacrifice anticipate the incarnation of Yeshua, they were a type of intercessory prayer crying out for Messiah to come and die for our sins. They were dramatic pleas in faithful expectation of the coming sacrifice of the Lamb of God that the world would be preserved and the nations saved. The sacrifices are a picture of our redemption in Messiah. He is the priest who consumes our sin so that it is absolved within his sacrifice, as the ancient priests once ate of the offering with its transferred sin and guilt. Today, we have fellowship with God in the bread and wine that represent Messiah's body and blood just as the ancient Israelites ate of the fellowship offering.

I believe that without the priestly work of God through Israel, the world would have been destroyed. I also believe that the hundreds of years of priestly intercession were a part of God's working to bring forth the Messiah.

Some fourteen hundred years of blood sacrifices called out for the coming of Yeshua! He came in the fullness of time. Is that fullness related to the adequacy of the intercession for his coming? All of the blood cried out for his coming over two times seven hundred years until the Temple was destroyed (seven being the number of perfection and ten times ten suggesting double completion), each sacrifice symbolically confirming Abraham's decision to sacrifice Isaac. As with Abraham, in every burnt offering the priests offered themselves and humanity back to God in submitted partnership. Were their hearts always right when they did this? Did they fully understand what they were doing? No, but they did it nevertheless and at various levels of heart faithfulness. Israel's history is not merely a footnote in salvation history, but an essential part of God's working, which brought forth Messiah and gave salvation to the world.

Temple Architecture and the Parallel in the High Priest

There are other dimensions as well to this priestly representation connected to the Temple. In his book, *Images of the Spirit,* Meredith Kline of Gordon-Conwell Theological Seminary has commented that the Temple ritual provides us with pictures of redemption and insights concerning the nature of humanity and the universe. For example, Israel is the Holy Land in the midst of the earth; Jerusalem is the holy city in Israel; Mount Zion is the holy place in Jerusalem and the Temple, the holy place on Zion. The Most Holy Place in the Temple completes the progression. This foreshadows the day when the whole earth will be holy, the Body of Messiah will be a holy temple, and each individual will be a temple of the Spirit. The tripartite division of the Temple is also a direct reflection of God's intended order for man. The outer court is like the physical body. The inner court is parallel to the soul which is the seat of emotion, will, and thought. The Most Holy Place (or Holy of Holies) is where the Spirit dwells in a born again person. The Spirit dwells in that most inner place of our being out of which springs our deepest intuitions and motivations.

The whole nation shows itself to be the priesthood since the nation was organized around the Temple. The tithes from the whole nation supported the Temple. Pilgrim journeys to Jerusalem gave a priestly role to all Israelites. So the people in the Land fit into the architecture of the Holy Land.

The High Priest is also a representation of the nature of redeemed humanity. The splendor of his garments shows us both the glory of God and the glory of man being restored in the image of God. Indeed, the High Priest is symbolic of Yeshua, the perfect High Priest who represents God and man. The priest's garments are a mirror image of the Temple. His outermost garments are parallel to the inner most part of the Temple and the nature of man. It contains the pouch with the Urim and Thummim for discerning the will of God (spiritual discernment). We discern the will of God in the inner spirit. Between the outermost garments and the inner garments are the colors of the Temple curtain, colors of fire and smoke veiling the Most Holy Place. Even so, the Holy Spirit, who is manifest as the pillar of fire and cloud in the Temple is to dwell in us and from our inner spirit bring the soul into a submission which can radiate the glory of God.

When the High Priest brought his sacrifice once a year into the Most Holy Place, he was the perfect symbolic representation of Yeshua's work. This was the pinnacle of Israel's annual Temple ritual on Yom Kippur, when atonement was made for the entire Nation of Israel on the only day in the year when ritual entrance to the Most Holy Place was permitted. That ritual showed the full symbolic power of the High Priest. In retrospect, it also clearly presents God's ultimate intention to restore his original, right relationship with all humanity through the atoning blood of Yeshua. Again, because Israel was called a nation of priests, the Day of Atonement ritual also was an intercessory act for the sake of the salvation of the world.

Ancient Israel played the essential role in the salvation history of preserving the world and blessing it with salvation by bringing forth Messiah. Their fourteen hundred year sojourn in the Land of Israel also established a Temple history, which is essential for understanding the full meaning of the sacrifice of Yeshua. The saved remnant of Israel, the Messianic Jew, is particularly called to keep this understanding alive, for the traditional and modern Jews do not fully understand the meaning of Israel's history or its contemporary practice.

A Pictorial Representation of God's Truth Through The Holy Days

Israel's priesthood and its Holy Days were directly linked by the sacrifices commanded by God to provide atonement and forgiveness for his people. All the Holy Days, all the "Appointed Times," included sacrifices because their redemptive importance for the Jewish people is based on sacrificial atonement and forgiveness. Beyond this, the Holy Days are pictures of truth concerning the nature of God and humanity, as well as a prophetic foreshadowing of the end of this age and the glory of the age to come.

When Israel carries out these celebrations, they are like intercessory prayers calling forth the manifestation of what is pictured. The practice of these traditional rites releases a spiritual power to move history toward the goal pictured in the symbolic actions. Because many Christians have not respected the Jewish roots of their faith, the full benefits of this spiritual legacy are not commonly known. The life and history of Israel is like a book that needs to be read for the benefit of our understanding. As we examine the Holy Days of Israel, we will see that the priestly oversight of the celebrations is not only for the benefit of Israel but also fulfils their calling to intercede for all nations.

The Calling of Israel in the Mosaic Covenant **17**

Sabbath

The Sabbath is the first and central appointed time in the life of Israel. It is unique as a weekly celebration. First, the Sabbath is a testimony to the nature of reality. The personal infinite God created the heavens and the earth in six days (*yamim*) and rested on the seventh day (*yom*). The Hebrew word "yom" can be taken as a 24-hour day or an age. God's rest on the seventh day does not connote that God was tired and needed to sleep. Rather, the burst of creative activity was over after six days. Resting is more like taking a step back and enjoying the work that has been done.

The Sabbath is a memorial of creation integrated into the weekly cycle of life to reflect the example set by God. Therefore, a Jew who keeps the seventh-day Sabbath proclaims that the God of Israel is the Creator. He confesses and proclaims over the whole earth that God is Lord over all. The existence of the Jew and the Sabbath proclaims: God Exists, God Exists, God Exists! The world is not the product of time plus chance plus matter, as in the theory of evolution. It is not the product of an unknowable vague pantheistic force. It is not the product of gods of nature. The Sabbath is both a profound testimony and a form of intercession that releases power toward the universal confession of the Lordship of God over all the earth.

As God rested on the seventh day, so we are to enter into rest. This aspect of the Sabbath is seen in the commandment given after the Exodus. The Jewish people were slaves in Egypt and suffered cruel bondage under complete, economic servitude. When Adam and Eve fell into sin, the ground was cursed and they were warned that economic survival would be their severe trial. The worst kind of economic bondage is found in slavery and Israel's history and identity is grounded in their deliverance out of slavery under the Egyptians and delivered into a promised land.

The Sabbath proclaims this liberation and is a weekly memorial of the Exodus. By resting one day in seven, Israel declares that the economic realm will not be the determining factor in their lives. They can take one day off in seven because God is the provider and will provide abundantly even if one seventh of life is given to worship, fellowship and celebration. Of course with the other designated times it is much more than one seventh. When we add in Sabbath years, we see that Israel was called to an extraordinary level of faith in God's provision instead of working in bondage to the economic realm. The Sabbath is proclaimed as a covenant sign for a way of life that honors God (Exod. 31:16, 17).

The Sabbath is also noteworthy for its humanitarian dimensions. In the Ten Commandments in Deuteronomy 5, we read that all are to be given the benefit of the rest of Sabbath, including animals, strangers, and the foreign slaves.

Israel's calling as priests to the nations also teaches us that Sabbath rest is a sign of the will of God for all peoples. It is God's intention that all be liberated from the bondage of slavery, both literally (externally) and spiritually (internally) from the soul bondage that destroys our peace and happiness. The Sabbath is a foreshadowing of the Age to Come and the universal Promised Land where all will live in the peace and rest of God. The Hebrew word "shalom" is a key term, defined as wholeness, peace, and well-being. By being reconciled to God and living by the power of his Spirit we enter into the rest of faith (Hebrews 4). The Sabbath foreshadows that one day all nations will enter into God's rest. Sabbath observance is an intercessory action for the sake of all nations, releasing the power of God to move history toward this goal.

The celebration of the Sabbath is part of the irrevocable call of God and a gift to Israel. It has been part of God's covenant order for Israel and is part of her on-going life today. This calling includes Messianic Jews, of course, who celebrate with full understanding because in Ye-shua, the *Sar Shalom* (Prince of Peace), we enter his rest. In this age, other people are free to join us in Sabbath celebration, but they are not required or given the seventh day Sabbath as their responsibility.

Although the Ten Commandments are mostly universal in application, as pointed out by Meredith Kline and others, and in Rabbinic thought, the commandments are in the form of a covenant given to Israel. This is shown by the words that begin the covenant, that God is the Lord that brought Israel out of Egypt (Exod. 20:1). The Sabbath is specifically a covenant sign given to the Nation of Israel within this covenant document. While there is no hint that the Gentiles during this age have such a covenant responsibility, the Sabbath day will become universal in the Millennium (e.g. Isaiah 66:23), there is no commandment that the Gentiles during this age have such a covenant responsibility.

Pesach (Passover)

The Exodus events are foundational to Israel's existence, so the month of the Exodus begins the lunar year for Israel. During the Passover feast (called a *Seder*), Israel remembers its great deliverance from Egypt and the events surrounding the Exodus. During the Seder celebration the plagues are recalled, the stubbornness of Pharaoh, the defeat of the Egyptian gods represented in the plagues, the miraculous deliverance through the sea, and the drowning of the Egyptian troops. The Passover lamb brought deliverance for Israel and the blood on the doorposts and lintels averted the judgment of the Angel of Death. That angel passed over the dwellings of the Israelites; hence the name Passover. After the Exodus, Israel was to conquer and enter the Promised Land.

In the New Covenant, Yeshua is our "Passover Lamb," in whom we find deliverance. This is emphasized in the Seder that Yeshua celebrates just before his crucifixion before the actual Feast. His fulfillment of the meaning of Passover is emphasized in all four Gospels.

Again, Passover proclaims the intent of God for all peoples. He desires that all be liberated from bondage and enter into a land of promise. Therefore, the Passover is both a representation for and a foreshadowing of the liberation of all peoples from tyranny and oppression through reconciliation with God.

God chose Abraham and then brought his descendants into Egyptian slavery. Was this a manifestation of his favor? Certainly in one sense, because it enabled Israel to fulfill her priestly calling of representation. God identifies with those who are oppressed and has declared his desire for their freedom. Israel's experience of suffering and deliverance is representative and for the sake of all those who suffer under oppression.

The Chosen People began their national life in slavery, and this has inspired countless others. The Pilgrims and Puritans looked to the Exodus of Israel for inspiration and believed they were following a similar, providential path as they crossed the Atlantic. Martin Luther King pointed to the Exodus as he led the Civil Rights movement in America. Many liberation movements look to the Exodus for hope. Through the encouragement of Rev. Kim Hansik, the nation of Korea celebrates the Korean Passover. They eat foods that remind them of their bondage during the war against communism and remember their oppression under the Japanese. As Korean Christians thank God for their liberation, they reflect on their recent history as a parallel experience to the Exodus.

The celebration of Passover looks forward to the day when the whole world will be liberated; Israel and the nations will be one under the rule of the Messiah. The whole world will be a Promised Land for all of the nations, and each one will receive due honor and respect. When done in faith, the celebration releases spiritual power to move history toward the biblical vision of Isaiah 2:3, when the world will learn the universal Torah of God in New Covenant application and live according to his ways as God's Word goes forth from Zion. More specific meanings that are present in the Passover-Exodus are presented in my books, *Jewish Roots* and *Israel, the Church and the Last Days*.

The Passover-Exodus is also prophetic of the last days before Yeshua returns. The Book of Revelation can be understood as a repetition of the Passover-Exodus on a worldwide scale. This time, the Pharaoh is the Antichrist. The plagues are poured out on an Egypt, which is the World. God's people are protected by the sealing of the Spirit (Revelation 7), so that the plagues do not hurt them (just as Israel was protected in the land of Goshen (see Exod. 8:18 (22); 9:26). God's people include the Jewish people and those from every tribe and nation (Rev. 7). There is an Exodus-like deliverance, although not through the sea, but into the Glory cloud as the rapture of the saints takes place (Rev. 11:15–18; 14:14–16). The armies of the Antichrist and the people who oppose God drown in the outpouring of his wrath (Rev. 19; Zech. 14). After this great exodus, the people of God enter into the Promised Age (Rev. 21).

The celebration of Passover consists of intercessory activities that move the world toward the redemptive events of the last days. That which is pictured in ceremony releases power toward its fulfillment. Prayers for world redemption are part of the seder. For Messianic Jews, Yeshua is the Passover Lamb who died to make atonement for our sins. He is the true prophet foretold by Moses (Deut. 18:15–19), leading us out of bondage and bringing us into a place of promise. He is King of Israel, our High Priest and King of all the earth.

Shavuot (Pentecost)

Shavuot or Pentecost, the next appointed time (fifty days after Passover), celebrates the first harvest. Since Israel is a land in a Mediterranean climate, there are two major harvests, one in the early summer and one in the fall. The harvest feasts, especially, proclaim God as the provider; in thanksgiving we praise him for all his bounty.

Though not noted in the Bible, Shavuot was recognized as the time of the giving of the Law, the Torah, from Mount Sinai, fifty days after the first Passover. But the feast is best known to Christians from the events recorded in Acts 2, when the Holy Spirit was first poured out on Yeshua's followers in Jerusalem. Empowered by the Spirit, the Apostle Peter led them to draw in the first great harvest of people (about 3,000) into the Kingdom both from Israel and from across the ancient Roman Empire.

There will be another great harvest at the end of the age. Shavuot, like Passover, ultimately looks forward to the time when all nations will submit to God's instruction, the Torah. For Messianic Jews, the Torah is the design of God for every area of human existence and includes the teaching of the whole Bible. The Torah will go forth from Zion. Yet how much more do we see that the Torah can only be lived out when it is written on our hearts! We cannot live out the Torah in its true meaning through our own efforts, but only by the power of the Spirit's work in us. We submit to the Spirit and can now obey (Jer. 31:31 ff.; Ezek. 36:24 ff.). Once again, Israel's celebration has an intercessory quality, anticipating that all nations will one day come to the truth that is being celebrated.

In the seventh month of the year, there are three major holy observances: *Yom Teruah*, the feast of sounding the *shofar* (ram's horn), which Jewish people called *Rosh Hashanah* (the New Year); *Yom Kippur* (the Day of Atonement); and *Sukkot* (the Feast of Tabernacles).

Yom Teruah (The Feast of Trumpets) and *Rosh Hashanah* (The New Year)

Yom Teruah takes place on the first day of the seventh month. Indeed the symbolism relates to its number: maturity, completion and perfection. The first day of each month is a New Moon and celebrates the faithfulness of God and new beginnings for his followers. Hence, the sounding of the shofar in the seventh month is a call to everyone in Israel to make a new beginning and to seek perfecting from God.

This new beginning will come to the whole world when "the last shofar" sounds and Messiah Yeshua returns in judgment and redemption. This feast is the background for understanding those future events (1 Thess. 4:16, 17; 1 Cor. 15:53ff.). The dead in the Messiah will rise first; then we who are alive will be caught up in the clouds to meet the Lord in the air. Believers will return with him as the judgments of Messiah purify the world. During this Holy Day, the blowing of the shofar is a prophetic proclamation calling the world to repentance and to prepare for the judgments of God as we prepare to enter the Age to Come. It is an intercessory act that calls for the Messiah's coming. While it summons the people of God to immediate rededication, it looks forward to the events of the last days.

Yom Kippur (Day of Atonement)

On Yom Kippur, the most holy day of the Jewish calendar, the High Priest made atonement for all Israel in the Most Holy Place. He sprinkled the blood of the sacrificial bull and a sacrificial goat on the cover of the Ark of the Covenant, which contained the tablets of the Law, the Ten Commandments. We have already noted the symbolism of the Temple and the garments of the High Priest.

This day proclaims, above all other days in Israel's calendar, that a blood substitute is needed for our sins. Yet the sacrifice of an animal is only a symbol of the real sacrifice, which was performed by our High Priest, Yeshua. He alone, as the Son of God, was able to bring his own blood, once and for all, into the Holy Place of Heaven to atone for the sins of Israel and the nations. Only his life, given in love for us, releases the power to cancel and overcome our sins. For the blood is life, and when Yeshua gave his life, he released the mighty power of his life for the sake of our reconciliation.

Hebrews 8 and 9 describe the wonderful and full meaning of Yom Kippur in Yeshua. However, for the meaning of Yom Kippur to be fulfilled, the atonement of Yeshua's blood must be applied to Israel and all of the nations of the world. This will reconcile the world to God and the nations to one another. All peoples will find forgiveness on every level; personal conflicts and ethnic conflicts will be settled. Zechariah 12–14 describes the events of the last days. It points to the time after the great judgments when Israel and the nations will receive the great atonement of Yeshua and be one under his rule (Zech. 12:10; 13:1ff. 14:9). These dimensions of Yom Kippur are still future.

The time between Yom Teruah and Yom Kippur are times that foreshadow the judgments and the wrath of God. This period of ten days between the two Holy Days is represented by the bowls of God's wrath in the book of Revelation, a sign of the world's need for the priestly intercession to which Israel has been called.

Once again, the larger meaning of the Holy Days is intercessory and is a sign that God will bring about all of the meanings foreshadowed in the celebrations. Such practices have the immediate meaning of recounting the events of salvation history and what God has done for us in the Messiah. They are a present witness and pattern for thanksgiving. However, they also move history toward the goals of God. Yom Kippur is an appropriate time to make explicit confessions in prayer and intercession for Israel and the nations.

All of these Holy Days are part of God's means of preserving the unique Nation of Israel for a unique testimony to the reality of God in the midst of the earth. They are pictures of eschatological, last days, events to come.

Sukkot (Tabernacles)

The Feast of Sukkot, marking the year's final harvest, is the last and greatest celebration of the year. It also begins during the seventh month with the appearance of the full moon, which provides the brightest evening light for communal festivities.

The time of harvest celebrations makes complete sense in the climate of Israel. This shows us how the biblical calendar is rooted in a particular people in a particular land. But even with the Jewish people scattered, the Land of Israel remains in them by the rhythm of this cycle of life.

Sukkot is important for its connections to the Kingdom of God and for the sacrifices offered for all the nations of the earth, the seventy bulls sacrificed according to the book of Numbers. It is a further example of Israel's life of intercessory mediation and activity for the sake of the nations of the world.

The location of Israel further communicates this witness. In one sense it was a dangerous location between empires, which would seek to control her territory. On the other hand, Israel was on the central trade root between three continents, Africa, Europe, and Asia. As such, it was uniquely located for spreading and establishing the truth of God.

The revelry at Sukkot was full of joy and delight. All Israelites are commanded to live in tents during the festival; Sukkot literally means "tents" in Hebrew. This is a celebration of thanks to God for the harvest and all his many gracious acts of provision. To heighten the Jewish people's awareness of their blessings in the land and their past dependence on God, Israel lives in tents as they did during the Exodus. That was when God provided supernatural food and drink, and clothes did not wear out. They were fed manna in the wilderness to remember that, "Man does not live by bread alone, but by every word that proceeds from the mouth of God" (Deut. 8:3). Once Israel was settled in their land with farms, homes and flocks, they were not to forget that God is the provider. They might be tempted to consider their wealth to be the fruit of their own labors. However, the source of all good things is God's gracious hand. Our efforts are only blessed when we are submitted in partnership with him; we must acknowledge him to be the One who gives us the ability and opportunity to succeed.

This symbolic reenactment is also a message to the whole world. Sukkot is a pilgrim festival. In ancient times, people came from all over the Land, dwelling in tents throughout the vicinity of Jerusalem, presenting the foreign traveler with an awesome sight. The message is that the whole world needs to come to God and repudiate their inheritance of independence since the Garden of Eden and Adam's fall. They need to return to the Father and find him as the provider for all their needs. Our security is not by the way of works, but by the way of grace.

Sukkot is a continual eight-day celebration. Seven days may represent the ages of this world and the eighth day celebrates the everlasting age. Thus it is an anticipation of the joyous, everlasting Kingdom in which all nations will submit to the rule of God and his Messiah-King. Zechariah 14:16 reveals the prophecy that all nations will come to Jerusalem to celebrate Sukkot in the Millennial Age. "On that day there will be one LORD, and his name the only name" (Zech. 14:9).

During the feast, Yeshua pointed to traditional rites in order to declare his calling as the one through whom to find the provision of God (John 7–9). In one of the climactic ceremonies on the last day of the Feast, the High Priest poured water brought from the Pool of Siloam into a basin next to the altar. Volleys of trumpets accompanied the ritual and sacred songs from the Levite musicians, while the people chanted from the psalms known as the Hallel (Pss. 113–118). Yeshua cried out during the ceremony: "If anyone is thirsty, let him come to me and drink and out of his inner most being shall flow rivers of living water" (John 7:37). In connection with the lighting of the lamps in the Temple courts, Yeshua said, "I am the light of the world" (John 8:12). Indeed, he is the light of God, which those lights were meant to represent. The Talmud states that the whole of Jerusalem was full of light when so many lamps were lit and it was glorious to behold (*Sukkah* 53a).

In all probability, Yeshua was born at the beginning of the Feast of Sukkot (figured by using the calculation of the courses of the priests and the birth of John the Immerser). His circumcision may well have been on the eighth day of the feast. There is a hint of this when John 1:14 states that Yeshua "tabernacled" among us. With so many pilgrims in Jerusalem and its environs for the feast, this may explain why accommodations were so full that Yeshua had to be born in a manger.

The annual cycle of traditions effectively demonstrates Israel's irrevocable calling to engage as an intercessory-representative for the redemption of the peoples of the earth. The gifts of God relate to the blessings of life in the Land. The call also includes Israel's priestly role in intercession and witness. This ancient nation, preserved by divine grace and faithfully holding to biblical traditions, has established the truth of God for all to see.

CHAPTER FOUR

HOW ANCIENT ISRAEL LIVED ITS CALLING

All the biblical dimensions of the life of Israel—the traditions, the Holy Days, the priestly sacrifices and regulations—are intertwined and make up one whole. We only separate these different aspects to gain a fuller understanding. An example of this integration can be seen in the Ten Commandments where the fourth command, concerning the Sabbath, is also a covenant sign between God and Israel. There is also no clear separation of the moral and ceremonial. The ceremonial serves both moral and representative purposes.

In that regard, it is particularly important that Israel's gifts and call emphasized living according to the character of God as reflected in his Torah. In looking forward to the Kingdom of God under Messiah, the New Covenant Scriptures highlight the universal aspects of the Torah as applicable in the New Covenant age.

By the time of Yeshua, the Pharisees were already distinguishing those dimensions of Torah that were universally applicable to all people in contrast to the aspects that were the sole responsibility of the Jewish people (Bockmuehl). The Mosaic Torah is not ideal in every case for all times and places. There are accommodations for the weakness of the people and the age in which it was given. Under the circumstances of fallen humanity and life in the ancient Middle East, God allowed for indentured bondage or slavery, for divorce and for polygamy. The permanent standards of God are also discernable and well reflected by the Mosaic writings.

In comparison to the legal systems of that time, there is an astonishing superiority and grace in the Torah. Indeed, life lived in accordance with the Torah is a good life, a humane life and qualitatively improved over any nation. It is a manifestation and a foreshadowing of the age of the Kingdom of God.

Mosaic legislation made all judges accountable to the Law of God. Neither was the king above the law, unlike in other lands. Judges were held responsible for rendering impartial and true decisions. In its humane quality, the Law is unparalleled. Every seventh year all debts were canceled and the Land lay fallow. This would renew opportunity for people who had setbacks and, consistent with good agricultural science, would also restore the Land. The need for food would be fulfilled by God's provision of an abundant harvest in the sixth year and by reaping whatever the land might produce on its own in the seventh.

The Torah required faith in God and his Word if it was to be obeyed. On the fiftieth year the land was not cultivated. Thus for two years the land was to lie fallow, the seventh sabbatical and the Jubilee. This required greater supernatural provision. On the fiftieth year all lands were to be returned to ancestral family owners. Land could not be sold in perpetuity, for God owned the Land. It could only be sold for the number of years left until the Jubilee. Since debts were canceled and land returned, all would have an opportunity for economic success.

The Torah included the command to love one's neighbor and to deal with those who fell into hardship with generosity. It required the punishment of violent criminals, rapists, idolaters, and occultists by death. These were capital crimes, repudiating the covenant itself. However, those who committed lesser crimes were to repent and make restitution under the supervision of the community. The penalty was to fit the crime. The Torah given through Moses includes righteous teaching intended for the judicial system and for government administrators. It includes high standards of personal morality. It includes guidance for international relations. All is based on the supreme commandment, to "Love *ADONAI* your God with all your heart, all your being and all your resources." (Deut. 6:5) and the love of one's neighbor (Lev. 19:18). The quality of life in Israel was to be a testimony to the nations. Sadly, many periods of Israel's history were full of compromise and the witness was limited. However, there were periods of faithfulness and great testimony. The days of Joshua and the elders who survived him, the monarchy of King David, and the early years of Solomon are worthy of mention.

The testimony of Israel was to embody love and justice because she was submitted to the God of love and justice, Creator of the universe.

> Look, I have taught you laws and rulings, just as *ADONAI* my God ordered me, so that you can behave accordingly in the Land where you are going in order to take possession of it. Therefore, observe them; and follow them; for then all peoples will see you as having wisdom and understanding. When they hear of all these laws, they will say, 'This great nation is surely a wise and understanding people.'(Deut. 4:5–8)

Life in the Kingdom was meant to reflect both the character and the power of God. If Israel obeyed the commands of God she would find the power of God operating in her life. This would also be a witness to the peoples of the earth. The promises were extraordinary. The people would experience none of the diseases which were put upon the Egyptians (Exod. 15:26). None of the Israelite women would miscarry. The people would live out the full span of human life (Exod. 23:26). In addition, there would be extraordinary prosperity from the land, in their industry and their fulfilled relationships. Deuteronomy 28 lists the marvelous blessings of obedience.

In addition, with regard to the nations, she would be the head and not the tail. Her enemies would come against her one way and flee in seven directions. Israel was to enter into no foreign alliances with the nations, for this entailed sharing the gods of the nations as was common practice in alliances. God would be her supernatural protection. In periods of Israel's faithfulness we find that the promises were significantly fulfilled. During the days of righteous King Jehoshaphat, the armies opposing Israel turned on one another while Israel's army sang praises. No arrow had to be shot, nor sword raised. That a small nation between empires would be free from being a vassal to any larger state would have been a miraculous testimony. It would prove the superiority of Israel's God over all other gods; that he is the only God over all the earth.

Of course, this testimony was limited. Israel failed and was taken into captivity as predicted in the Mosaic writings. Every aspect of the nation's captivity and eventual return to the land was equally a manifestation of God's power and sovereignty. But the great prophetic voices of God were already looking forward to a greater promise, a New Covenant for Israel that would write the Law on their hearts and move them to obey his statutes, ordinances, and judgments. All would *know* the Lord with an intimacy that implied direct, personal relational knowledge (Jer. 31:31ff. Ezek. 36:25 ff.).

Furthermore, God reaffirmed his promise to the nation: a promise of redemption, security and the assurance of dwelling in the land of Israel without fear of being uprooted. But this prophetic vision of Israel's redemption did not lose sight of the original covenantal promise to Abraham. Israel's calling will be ultimately fulfilled in the redemption of all the nations of the world (Isa. 2:1ff. Isa. 11:1ff.). Indeed, their redemption will surely take place because of God's promise to redeem his people, Israel.

In summary, Israel was called to establish a nation in the midst of the earth that has preserved and lived out the truth of God. Their life under the Lord shows the significance of God's Word, his standards, and his redemption. Neither their failures nor their exile have prevented God from carrying out his loving, perfect will enfolded in his redemptive purpose.

Chapter Five

Israel's Calling in a Transitional Age

After the death and resurrection of Yeshua, followed by the outpouring of the Spirit on the Feast of Shavuot, the Kingdom of God arrived to a greater degree than ever before. Although Israel had experienced the Spirit dwelling in the Most Holy Place of the Temple, and in chosen leaders and prophets, in the era of the New Covenant every individual disciple had become a temple of the Holy Spirit (1 Cor. 3:16; 6:19).

Israel's Failed Expectations

After centuries of battling successive waves of conquering armies, Israel had expected Messiah to deliver them from their enemies. In the first century, the Jewish people combined religion and violent zeal to resist Roman oppression. In the popular spiritual visions of Yeshua's day, God would pour out his wrath on the nations and initiate such a mighty deliverance of Israel that the blindness of the nations would be removed, and all would stream into the Kingdom of God (Isa. 25–27). Israel would become the capital of the nations and the Word of the LORD would go forth from Zion (Isa. 2:3). The whole world would prosper under the rule of the Messiah and Israel would finally and completely fulfill her calling.

Israel's Messianic expectations did not anticipate an age of transition in which salvation would be offered to the Gentiles before the age to come. However, God made his intentions clear through the first generation of Jewish apostolic leaders (Acts 10, 13–15). With the emergence of a New Covenant people that included both Jew and Gentile, the Body of the Messiah was formed.

The first new fellowships of Jew and Gentile were rooted in Israel under Jewish apostolic authority (Acts 15). Among that leadership, many of whom gave us the New Covenant Scriptures, we see that Israel's call from God was commonly affirmed. Yet, by the end of the second century, when Gentiles dominated the Body of Messiah, most Christians had little understanding of the continuing gifts and call of God to Israel.

In the centuries that followed, Christian theology diminished and then denied any continuing role for Israel in God's purposes, replacing it with the Church. These views have only begun to change since the

Reformation with the growth of Bible-centered Christian movements. But many continue to insist that the call of ethnic Israel came to an end with the creation of the Church. Some have suggested that the institution of the New Covenant implies this. Others believe that Israel lost her spiritual status due to sin. In addition, it is argued that even if there is such a call, the Jewish believer has no part in it.

As a result, many essential questions and issues about the call of Israel need a new, wider discussion throughout the Body of Messiah. Since the whole Church is a Kingdom of priests (1 Pet. 2:5, 9), what is the continuing priestly role for the Nation of Israel? Is the saved remnant of Israel, the Jewish believer in Yeshua, part of this continuing call? How does the call of Jewish believers in Yeshua differ from their fellow Jews?

Fortunately, Jewish groups of believers from the first and early second century have left us a great legacy of authoritative texts and testimony on these issues. The apostles themselves established the theology of these groups. This is why there is universal scholarly agreement that the apostolic consensus, as reflected in Matthew 5:17–19, was that Jewish disciples of Yeshua were called to maintain a life of Jewish commitment. There has been some doubt on Paul's view of the matter, but today he is commonly interpreted as fully in accord with this consensus. All the believers remain under apostolic authority. Hence the apostolic position must be our position. This leads to further questions. How are Jew and Gentile distinguished in the body of believers? Are their priesthoods the same or different?

The Call on Israel in Unbelief

Paul was grieved to admit in his letter to the congregation in Rome that Israel had largely rejected their Messiah. Yet he emphasized that this was not the end of divine favor: "God did not reject his people whom he foreknew" (Rom. 11:2). Even in unbelief, the Jewish people can't help but testify to the truth of the Scriptures. In their dispersion, but also by their preservation in the midst of the nations, Scripture continues to be fulfilled (Lev. 26, Deut. 28).

What other nation has been preserved despite so many recurring tragedies and repeated attempts to destroy their race? This is amazing evidence for the whole world, a proof that equally makes all nations accountable to the Word of God. Tragically, Israel's suffering throughout her history matches the descriptions of the dispersions foretold by the prophets and also by Yeshua, who spoke of Jerusalem being trodden down by the Gentiles "until the age of the Goyim [Gentiles] has run its course." (Luke 21:24). In his mercy, God gave periods of Jewish prosperity in some lands, but ultimately persecution again flared up as God allowed Satanic outbreaks of anti-Semitism. The attitude and behavior of the Christian institutions and churches in the nations where Jewish people have lived over the centuries has also been a means of God's testing and judging both the churches and those nations.

The post-World War II re-gathering of the Jewish people back to the Land of Israel, without the majority being followers of Yeshua, is also in accord with the Word of God (Butler). Never in history has a nation been so restored. The eerie visions of Ezekiel 37, dry bones without life, regathered and renewed with flesh and blood, accurately depict the familiar black and white newsreel scenes of concentration camp horrors that sent the survivors fleeing to Israel. As the prophet foresaw, God has chosen to reconstitute them as a nation before he puts his Spirit in them. In Zechariah 12 we also find confirmation that the Jewish people are to be in the land before they confess their Messiah (Zech. 12:10).

Throughout the centuries that span Israel's *Diaspora* and their re-gathering back to the Promised Land, we see that the gifts and call of God have continued through the nation as a witness to the truth of God's word.

Israel's continued faithfulness to the Sabbath and the Holy Days maintains a picture of redemption and spiritual truth for the world's benefit. One might say that Israel is in unbelief and blindness concerning key meanings of her practice. Nevertheless, the ritual imagery portrayed is still valid. Indeed, an actor may play the role of a great biblical character without believing in the Bible, yet audiences are affected; some even embrace the Good News. Orthodox Jews believe that the Hebrew Scriptures are the Word of God even if they do not fully understand it. If their practice is reflective of Hebrew scriptural thought, then it is still a rich resource for all.

Though Jewish people do not engage in literal sacrifices, the liturgy of the Jewish worship services is still done with direct reference to the practices of the ancient Temple. The same basic meanings instilled from the Hebrew Scriptures continue to be reflected in Jewish life. The irrevocable call—to act in an intercessory-representative role for humanity—continues, though in a weakened form without the vivid practices of the Temple. Ultimately, that weakness comes from the inability to see Yeshua's fulfillment of what was practiced. He is much greater than the shadow or the foreshadowing. Nevertheless, much of the meaning and depth of biblical teaching is still projected in Jewish life. There are also some Orthodox Jews who fully comprehend their life and practice (their call) as a means of intercession for the redemption of the World.

Does the intercessory element still continue though the nation is in unbelief? I believe that it does, but it is debatable. So far as Israel's practice illustrates the redemption of the world and the judgments of the last days, these are grounded in Scripture. That is why so much Jewish liturgy is simply a repetition of Scripture. Even in partial unbelief, Israel speaks the Word of God and this Word will not return void. There is still power released that moves history toward the goal of the fullness of the Kingdom of God on earth. Therefore, the priestly intercessory role can still be perceived in the unbelieving nation, though not at its full potential. Indeed, the experience of Messianic Jews is that with faith in Yeshua a much greater intercessory power is released through Jewish life.

While Israel is a representative nation among the nations, the Church is a representation from all nations. Before Yeshua returns there must be an adequate remnant from every nation, for "And this Good News about the Kingdom will be announced throughout the whole world as a witness to all the *Goyim*. It is then that the end will come." (Matt. 24:14). "End" here means the end of this age and the inauguration of the age to come. In priestly representation, the Church cries *maranatha,* "Come, Lord." This adequate representation will bring the judgments of the last days and the return of Yeshua. When the Church cries "maranatha" they must do so in unity to effectively call for the Lord to come and rule all nations.

However, there is also a nation, Israel, in the midst of the earth, which is literally a priestly representative of all the nations. This nation has been specifically instructed that it must call out to Yeshua to come and rule. Therefore, another aspect of Israel's call is to cry out for the coming of Messiah Yeshua. The onus lies on the leadership of the nation, as depicted in Yeshua's words addressing Jerusalem, a euphemism for the leadership: "Yerushalayim! Yerushalayim! you will not see me again until you say, 'Blessed is he who comes in the name of *ADONAI*'" (Matt. 23:37–39).Thus, in this age the climax of intercessory representation in Israel's redemptive purpose is to call upon Yeshua and invite him to rule Israel and the nations.

CHAPTER SIX

THE MESSIANIC JEWISH CALLING TODAY

The practice of Messianic Jews, the saved remnant of Israel, to live out their lives within their community, is a further proof of God's continuing covenant with the Nation of Israel as a whole. Messianic Jews live and practice the traditions with the full understanding of their fulfillment in Yeshua, a redemptive foreshadowing of the last days and the Age to Come. Only the Jewish follower of Yeshua, through the fullness of the Spirit and faith, can fully express the intercessory meanings of the Feasts and Jewish practices in Yeshua. Only they can release the full power of Israel's call. In this they are fully part of their people. Whatever can be said concerning God's gifts and calling for the Nation of Israel is equally true of the saved remnant of Israel, the Messianic Jews. The Jewish followers of Yeshua are still part of Israel and are also Jewish members of the "one new man," the Church. The Jewish believers, by maintaining their Jewish identity and traditions, keep alive the authentic context for understanding the Scriptures. They are visible evidence that the gift and call of God to the Nation of Israel, from Abraham to Yeshua, still continues.

The Apostle Paul points to his own faith as proof that the nation has not been rejected. He also affirms that this "remnant, chosen by grace" (Rom. 11:5) is proof that God has not rejected the nation as a whole. Paul applies here the principle of corporate representation: the whole may be sanctified by a righteous remnant. His argument also refers to a common sacrifice: when part of the dough offered as first-fruits is holy then the whole batch is holy (Rom. 11:16–24).

At the Jerusalem Council (Acts 15), held at the behest of Paul and Barnabus who were seeing unexpected success in ministry among the Gentiles, the Apostle James declared that Gentiles were free from the extensive ordinances of Jewish life. The apostle asked only that they hold to the primary, well-accepted requirements for God-fearers, sometimes known as the Noahic Covenant. He also noted that the Torah was publicly read for them every week in the synagogues. At this time, the Jewish disciples of Yeshua were still in the synagogues. The expectation was that the Gentiles would learn from Jewish practice, sometimes joining with them as led by the Spirit and would appreciate the full meaning of the Scriptures.

There was, of course, never any thought that Jewish followers of Yeshua would not continue to live as Jews. Jewish life proclaims that God exists and he will rule the whole world. Every time a Jewish person keeps the Sabbath and the Feasts, the Appointed Times, they proclaim the reality of God and look forward to the fullness of redemption to come when the Messiah will rule all nations. In its faithfulness to Torah and scriptural instruction, Jewish life continues to reflect a threefold meaning by its practice: first, pictures of redemption and spiritual truth; second, prophetic actions that call forth that which they portray; and third, intercessory activity for the sake of world redemption.

When Jewish followers of Yeshua celebrate the Sabbath and the Feasts, their practice shows a fullness of meaning not accessible to the traditional Jew who does not know the Lord. Therefore, the Jewish disciple who keeps these practices is a testimony to the reality of the God of Israel, he or she further affirms the nature of the Last Days and the Age to Come with greater power, understanding, and meaning, grounded in the person of Messiah Yeshua. A Jewish believer who abandons Jewish life testifies that Israel is not significant and that they are not part of the nation.

Jewish believers are not only the organic link between Israel and the Church; they foreshadow the unity of Israel and the Church through faith in the Messiah. In that ultimate unity, the whole Nation of Israel will be within the Body of Messiah while still being the Nation of Israel. Until that fulfillment takes place, the Messianic Jew plays a necessary role, for as Paul points out (Rom. 11: 5, 14) an identifiable remnant of Israel will be saved before all Israel is saved.

Biblical Zionism: Affirming Israel's Gift of The Land

Messianic Jews are Biblical Zionists. They believe, based primarily on the promises of God to the patriarchs, Abraham, Isaac and Jacob, that the ancient land of Israel belongs in perpetuity to the Jewish people, and that all Jews have the right to return there. Indeed, the promise of Israel's return to the Land is persistently repeated throughout the Bible. The first example is the Exodus from Egypt under Moses, and Israel's prophets repeated that expectation over the next thousand years.

Christian Zionism, based on a literal interpretation of the prophetic Biblical texts, became prevalent in England and the United States during the 19th century. The movement influenced some of the prominent English political leaders who supported the 1917 Balfour Declaration, declaring a Jewish homeland in Palestine.

After the Holocaust, the world recognized the just cause of the Jewish people. Most of the member nations of the United Nations had already proven that they could not protect the rights of their Jewish minorities. In light of Jewish historical suffering, aside from any reference to God's promise, Israel had every right to have their own country in their own land. It is one of the outstanding claims of justice in history and ought to be well recognized by the whole world.

In 1948 the U.N. voted to form the state of Israel and give the Jews their own state on land they reclaimed from desolation, as well as land purchased from Arab owners. Two of the wars fought after this decision led to border changes. The 1948 War of Independence was an outright attack on the fledgling nation within hours of its coming into existence. The 1967 Six Day War came after the armies of Egypt and Syria were massed on Israel's borders, and the Egyptian president ordered U.N. peacekeepers to leave the area. Throughout history, justice was played out this way: the aggressor rightly lost land and was penalized if defeated in war. This principle of historic justice has been ignored by numerous U.N. resolutions against Israel.

Some claim that the Palestinians were unjustly displaced from land that they occupied for hundreds of years. It is crucially important to unmask this deception. First, we must ask, at what point do a people cease to have any claim on their land after they have been dispossessed? Can people justly take back their land in ten years? Most would say, yes. What about fifty or five hundred years? No absolute right is given to keep possession of lands obtained by expelling the original occupants, even after many years.

In fact, only a small proportion of Israeli land was gained by removing Palestinians. From the 1880's to 1948, the Jews returned to a desolate region that was sparsely populated and purchased the land for their settlements. No land taken by force was part of the original U. N. mandated State of Israel. State-owned land passed from the Turkish Empire to Britain and then to Israel. In the 1948 and 1967 wars, Israel did displace some Palestinian occupants, but many of these were for security reasons.

In her classic study, *From Time Immemorial*, Joan Peters debunks the idea that most Palestinians are from long-term landed descendants. She uses census figures from the Turkish Empire to show that the vast majority of the Palestinians are recent 20th century immigrants to the Land. Only a minority are descendants of an historic people of the land.

The Palestinians do have one important justice claim. It is the claim of the stranger in the midst of Israel. They are to be treated generously and with justice. However, this refers to those people who are willing to live there peaceably and who can accept that God has given the Land to the Jews. This does not refer to people that seek to destroy the Jewish State! The big justice issues are all on the side of Israel (we could refer to them as macro-justice issues). The Palestinians can rightly claim the micro-justice issues as "strangers in the midst." Often the media only emphasizes the micro-justice issues, which produces a terribly distorted picture.

In addition, very little is ever said about the forced migration of some half-million Jewish refugees displaced by Israel's neighboring Arab countries. These countries used the creation of a Jewish state to rid themselves of historic and often prosperous Jewish populations. These Jewish refugees have long since integrated into Israel's population. A similar number of Palestinians were displaced at the birth of the state of Israel, but they are denied citizenship in other Arab countries, especially those rich in oil. Yet Palestinian refugees continue to be offered the promise of arms and violent ideology—sometimes nationalist, sometimes Islamic—to wipe out the Zionist state.

Why is the world so opposed to Israel? For Arabs, the primary issue is not empathy for Palestinian losses. The issue is spiritual, for in Islamic teaching any land that was under Muslim government must always be considered Muslim. The loss of Jerusalem strikes at the heart of the pride of Islam and contradicts the view that Islam has superseded Judaism and Christianity. The rest of the world wants to have peace by appeasing the Muslim world. This is sheer foolishness. They fail to realize that Islam's intentions for world conquest cannot be appeased. All the nations seek a world order that excludes the God of the Bible, who is the God of Israel. But God will not allow this. Israel, even in her unbelief challenges this view, but will fulfill that role completely when she comes into her fullness of faith through Messiah Yeshua.

The Messianic Jew and the Return to Israel

The return of our people to the Land of Israel from the end of the 19th century to the present, and the 1948 founding of the State of Israel, are among the most significant evidences of the truth of the Word of God. This is part of our calling: to be such a witness. Living in the Land of Israel is also part of our irrevocable gift and calling (Rom. 11:29).

This raises an important question. Should Messianic Jews make *aliyah* (return to live in Israel)? Some Israeli Messianic Jews assert that Jewish believers who live in the Diaspora are not fulfilling their calling. In my view, living in the Land of Israel should be the preferred orientation of Messianic Jews. The assumption should be to live there unless God has clearly led otherwise. However, God may clearly lead otherwise. As long as there are significant numbers of Jews in the Diaspora, Messianic Jews are needed in those communities. Though Israel has a significant claim upon us, the Spirit may delay the fulfillment of that claim. It is also clear to me that the prophetic picture in Scripture shows a great return to the Land before the return of the Messiah but also a return to the Land after his Second Coming.

Messianic Jewish participation in the return to the Land of Israel is an important prophetic and intercessory action. It is part of moving history toward the fulfillment of the Age to Come. The concept of land inheritance connects us to the physical importance of place as part of who we are as human beings. The doctrine of the Resurrection commits us to believe in a continued physical existence that connects us to the earth, whether in the Millennial Age or in the ultimate New Heavens and New Earth.

The Messianic Jewish presence in the Land is a foreshadowing of Israel coming to faith and peace in Messiah under the rule of *Sar Shalom*, the Prince of Peace. It also challenges the believers to show with their lives the reality of Scripture and their commitment to bring the promise of blessing to the Land of Israel.

Tensions are still common between Messianic Jews and the State of Israel. The Interior Ministry sometimes persecutes Messianic Jews, applying the Supreme Court decision stating that a Jew (by *halakhah*, the traditional Jewish law, one born of a Jewish mother and raised as a Jew) loses the right to return to the Land if he or she converts to another religion. Believing in Yeshua has been explicitly noted as a disqualifying religious conversion. Yet, the Interior Ministry has allowed many Messianic Jews to come and settle without pursuing them. However, there are anti-Messianic organizations that put pressure on employers to fire Messianic Jews. They also have picketed Messianic Jewish business owners and congregations and singled out individuals. Even so, there are significant religious freedoms in Israel. Most important, Messianic Jews and Messianic congregations are significantly growing in numbers. Of course, Jews who were raised in Israel and become Messianic Jews do not lose any rights. Descendants of

Jews (with at least one Jewish grandparent) continue to have the rights of citizenship.

The Messianic Jews are a righteous remnant in Israel. Their presence sanctifies the Nation as Romans 11 implies. Is the Messianic Jewish presence in Israel a key to Israel's preservation? Is it one of the sources of intercession for God's mercy on a people who are subjected to so many violent attacks? I believe so. We Messianic Jews have a priestly calling to minister to our own Jewish brothers and sisters; we are a key to the fulfillment of the destiny of the Jewish people in our land. Despite all the difficulties that confront us in Israel, aliyah should be an important consideration for Messianic Jews.

CHAPTER SEVEN

A CALLING TO HEAL

In looking back over Church history, it would be accurate to say that the Jewish people, through their Messiah and the faithful Jewish apostles that carried his message into the world, gave birth to the Church. So, too, the Church has been called to be the womb of intercession for affecting the rebirth of the Jewish people. However, there is a humbling dilemma; the historic Church has failed abysmally to fulfill her God-ordained role for Israel. The Church has been infected with the very anti-Semitism she was called to battle. The history of the Church's complicity in anti-Semitism and in crimes against the Jewish people is one of the great tragedies of history.

John Dawson, in his book *Healing America's Wounds*, calls anti-Semitism the greatest wound in all of history. He believes that reconciliation between Israel and the Church will release the power of God for the greatest evangelistic impact that the world has ever seen. Dawson presents a strong case for a ministry of reconciliation between conflicting ethnic groups through their representatives in the Church. There are many historic wounds between peoples: African Americans and European Americans, Japanese and Koreans, Serbians and Croatians, Arabs and Jews, and countless others. These inherited conflicts have sustained cycles of violence and bitterness over many generations, giving power to spiritual principalities that resist the message of God's Good News.

Dawson has initiated prayer gatherings where Christian representatives from opposing national groups meet together. They listen to one another's stories, gain a new perspective on their differences, and then wait on the Lord. The outcome for each group is repentance for their sins and forgiveness for the sins done against them over many years of conflict. When there is significant participation from opposing groups, Dawson has later seen a major advance of the Good News. Historically, believers identify with the cause of their ethnic group. However, God has given us the ministry of reconciliation. In meeting together, believers are empowered to act as priests on behalf of their own community, applying the blood of Yeshua to atone for the guilt and shame that are the consequence of inherited wrong attitudes and sinful behavior.

On the basis of Dawson's principles, reconciliation between Israel and the Church requires that Jewish believers meet with representatives of the Church. Only the Jewish followers of Yeshua can participate in both important roles: first, representing those who have historically suffered, and second, applying the blood of the Lamb in forgiveness and reconciliation.

This ministry of reconciliation, in keeping with the call of Israel as priestly intercessors for humanity, adds another dimension to the specific call of Jewish believers to act in an intercessory role for all Israel. It is a crucial form of intercessory representation. When I shared this with John Dawson, both in correspondence and in person, he immediately grasped that it is the same principle that is applied in his process to bring healing between other opposed communities.

These concerns began to be addressed as part of an effort called Toward Jerusalem Council II. An amazing board of seven Jews and seven Gentiles was formed. This board was committed to work toward a council or councils whereby the Church and its different denominational forms would officially embrace Messianic Jewish communities as showing the truth that Jews who believe in Yeshua are called to identify and live as Jews.

In order to move toward this goal, the board sponsored many prayer journeys over a ten-year period. We traveled with groups of intercessors representing many streams of the Church. Acts of intercessory repentance were made at the sites where Church decisions were made rejecting the Jews and rejecting Jewish believers in Yeshua. This included several sites in Spain: Elvira near Granada, Alhambra Palace in Granada, and Cordoba. It included Rome, Nicea, Antioch, Jerusalem, and Yavneh in Israel. Finally after ten years, in the fall of 2006, intercessors and leaders gathered in Jerusalem from 35 nations and every major denomination and stream of the Church. A significant contingent of Messianic Jews from Israel and the Diaspora joined them. Repentance, intercession, and worship characterized the gathering. There was a sense of great spiritual breakthrough.

There has never been such a significant gathering of representatives from different streams of the Church in unity with Messianic Jewish leaders. They came together to heal historic wounds and repudiate ancient decisions by the Church against Messianic Jews. The negative attitudes and prejudices, which led the Church Fathers to publicly exclude and then reject the Messianic Jews in the early centuries of Church history, had never been dealt with in such a convocation.

They also prayed concerning the decision of the rabbis at Yavneh, who oversaw the Jewish community after the fall of Jerusalem (70 C.E.) and acted to exclude the remaining Jewish believers (*"minim,"* or *Notzrim,* Nazarenes) from worshipping with the surviving Jewish community. Around the year 90 C.E. (some claim the decision took place a generation later, after the Bar Kokhba revolt), a curse on the minim was inserted into the regular daily prayers. Isolated from both the Gentile churches and their own ethnic community, the Nazarenes eventually disappeared.

In order to weigh the importance of these meetings, consider the views of a Catholic priest, Dr. Peter Hocken, who wrote a monumental volume called *The Glory and the Shame*. A charismatic Catholic, Dr. Hocken believed that the outpouring of the Spirit is, among other things, for the unity of the Church. However, he noticed that these divisions were only partially overcome in various revivals. Why?

Hocken argues that the Church will remain cursed with division until it deals with its relationship with Israel. Moreover, the Church cannot deal with Israel adequately until it confronts the modern Messianic Jewish movement. Hocken notes that the first Church division came from a rejection of the legitimacy of the early Messianic Jewish community. That decision established the roots of anti-Semitism and was repeatedly confirmed by the Church throughout the centuries. The Messianic Jewish movement provides the churches with an opportunity to redefine this history by alignment with and support of the contemporary Messianic Jewish movement. Hocken insists that this has to include prophetic acts of repentance and reconciliation. He also affirms Messianic Judaism as a self-governing and indigenous movement, which allows it to play a similar role with all denominations and streams of the Church. Finally, he suggests that doctrinal differences within the Church can likely be bridged by a return to the Jewish roots and context of our faith.

We can learn a great deal from a better understanding of the early Church's relationship with the original Messianic Jewish sects. In the first century, under the Apostles' leadership, the Jewish believers were respected as the parent elders of the Church. After the first century, however, the attitude of Gentile Church leaders began to change. The destruction of Jerusalem and the scattering of the Jewish people, along with Roman disdain for the Jews after the violent revolts against the empire, fostered the worst prejudices. The Jews were seen as cursed by God and the irrevocable call of Israel was denied. The Church was identified as the new Israel, fully replacing the old Israel.

Historians have shown that there were two streams of Jewish sects that embraced Yeshua as Messiah. The Ebionites were heretical and rejected the writings of Paul and parts of the Gospels; they also denied the deity of Yeshua. The other stream, the Nazarenes or Notzrim, accepted the deity of Yeshua and the whole New Covenant. Both groups were equally marginalized. Justin Martyr, the well-known early Christian writer, accepted that the Nazarenes were saved but voiced a widely held view: "He who would be both Christian and Jew can be neither Christian nor Jew." Yet some of the Nazarenes were descended from Yeshua's own family!

Later Church fathers denied that the Nazarenes were saved and claimed that living a Jewish life in Yeshua is heresy. This decision was canonized at the Council of Nicea II (787 C.E.) and reaffirmed in Church history until the middle of the nineteenth century. When a Jew professed faith in Yeshua, he was required to renounce the Jewish people, forsake all Jewish practices, adopt a Christian name and eat pork. Documents were signed according to these tenets. (This history and copies of such documents are reproduced in Schoenfeld's *History of Jewish Christianity*). This was a profound sin. The very descendants of those who gave the Gentiles liberty not to become Jews in practice were barred from their calling and identity. Indeed, the Jewish people were the only ethnic group in Church history denied their own identity. Because a Jewish believer was no longer Jewish, they had to assimilate into other ethnic groups.

The anti-Semitism that followed remains a distressing legacy for the Church. In the fifth century C.E., Chrysostom describes the Jews as veritable devils. The Crusaders considered killing the Jews to be a godly act of faithfulness to Yeshua. They killed vast numbers on the way to the Holy Land and thousands in Jerusalem. Luther railed publicly and in print against the Jews. Jewish believers who were found keeping the Passover or other Jewish practices were burned at the stake for heresy. These terrible sins not only severely wounded the Jewish people but also those who did the wounding.

On the other hand, the Jewish community agreed that one must choose to be a Christian or a Jew and denied the Jewish identity of the Messianic Jews. In the gathering of rabbis at Yavneh in Israel around 90 C.E., Samuel ha-Katan added a curse on heretics, which included the followers of Yeshua. This phrase was added to the lengthy prayer that the congregation reads while standing called the *Amidah*, or Eighteen Benedictions. Since the Jewish believers would not stand during this prayer, they were identified and cast out of the synagogues.

Tragically, both the Church and the Synagogue have rejected the organic link between them, the Messianic Jews. Until they recognize this link, full reconciliation between them is impossible. While initiatives such as Jewish-Christian dialogue are popular and well regarded, they cannot succeed in promoting real change. Ironically, Messianic Jews are usually denied involvement in this dialogue by both sides. Christians who want a friendly relationship with the Jewish community feel they must exclude Messianic Jews. We can understand the historic reasons for this. However, when Christians refuse to acknowledge the Jewish component in the Body of Messiah and do not want to share the full potential of reconciliation through the blood of Yeshua, they are making a major error.

It is incumbent on Christians to give themselves in witness, prayer and finances to help establish the Messianic remnant of Israel and to restore their place of honor in the Church.

Implications From Malachi 4

The last verses from the prophet Malachi are a compelling and powerful word of promise: "Look, I will send to you Eliyahu the Prophet before the coming of the great and terrible Day of *ADONAI*. He will turn the hearts of the fathers to the children and the hearts of the children to their fathers; otherwise I will come and strike the land with complete destruction" (Mal. 4:5, 6). Some contemporary leaders have discerned in Malachi 4:6 some larger implications from the reconciliation between literal fathers and children. Just as scholars have seen in the fifth commandment to "Honor your father and mother" an implied concern to honor all authority, these verses in Malachi can also be applied in a wider sense.

A vision of the hearts of fathers turning to their children and the hearts of children turned to their fathers is also relevant in the context of the Jewish people and the Church. The Church needs to honor her Jewish spiritual parents. Though the Church may consider the Jewish people as "missing it" with regard to Yeshua, it is still appropriate to act as a respectful child to parents who do not yet believe. Honoring its spiritual parentage is crucial for the Church to come into right order, understanding and unity. As Dr. Peter Hocken points out, the doctrinal corrections that are the key to Church unity will come from reading the New Testament according to a Jewish context.

It is equally important for the Jewish people to see the Church as their own offspring, even if it appears to be a wayward child. Only Messianic Jews can fully appreciate the need for this. Therefore, they intercede for Israel as a child would pray intensely for their parents to come to know Ye-shua and fulfill their destiny in righteousness. Messianic Jews are charged to pray for the Body of Messiah, a child of Israel, for unity, restoration, power, purity, effectiveness, and a Jewish-rooted understanding. They bear concern for the whole Church of born-again believers. Indeed, many in the Church pray this way, but the prayers of Messianic Jewish believers are essential for these efforts to succeed. Messianic Jews know that unless the Church fulfills its call and destiny, Israel will not be saved and world re-demption will not come. Gentile believers also understand that without the Messianic Jewish movement coming into its full strength and playing its proper role within Israel and the Body of the Messiah, the hope of world redemption cannot be fulfilled.

Israel and the Church are interdependent and fulfill different but complementary priestly roles. Without the Messianic Jews, who are part of both, neither can be fulfilled in their destiny. The Jews are dependent on God's work through the Gentiles for their salvation and the Gentiles are dependent on God's work through the Jews. This follows from the conclusion of Romans 11 where Paul has described the priestly call of the Gentiles to the Jews and the priestly call of the Jews to the Gentiles: "For God has shut up all mankind together in disobedience, in order that he might show mercy to all." (Rom. 11:32).

I believe that this suggests another picture. Before we enter into the everlasting ages, the Jewish believer will say to the Gentile in Messiah, "I honor you because without your prayers and faithfulness, I would never have been saved." The Gentile will respond, "Without your faithfulness in preserving the Scriptures, Jewish life, and taking the Good News into the world, I would not have been saved." They will revere one another with a humility that truly honors God and affirms that our faith is founded on interdependence.

Ultimately, the end of this age and the last wars described by the prophets, both spiritual and physical, will not occur until the Jewish be-lievers and the rest of the Church are right with each another. An ad-equate witness must be given to all the nations and equally given to Jewish people by the Church and Messianic Jews. Only then will Israel, with an anguished heart, call upon Yeshua for salvation. The thrilling ac-count is found in Joel 3, Zechariah 12 and 14 and Revelation 19. Israel will say, "Blessed is he who comes in the name of *ADONAI*." (Matt. 23:39). "Every knee will bow... and every tongue will acknowledge that Yeshua the Messiah is *ADONAI*..." (Phil. 2: 10,11).

CHAPTER EIGHT

OUR CALLING IN THE AGE TO COME

There is a destiny for Israel and the Church that they are bound to fulfill. For the Church, it is to rule as the Bride Queen by Messiah's side in the age to come. For Israel, it is to be the chief of the nations. Jerusalem is to be the world capital where Yeshua reigns visibly on his throne, the true seat of the United Nations of the Messiah. The Messianic Jew will participate in both of these.

There will be an age described by the prophets in which people can expect to live to a ripe old age (as in the pre-Flood era), and love and worship the Father and Yeshua. The knowledge of the Lord will cover the earth as the waters cover the seas (Isaiah 11:9). This will be a flourishing age with wonderful marriages that are fruitful with children, generations blessed with excellent health without the fear of disease and relieved from the burdens of accidental tragedy. Such is the indication in Isaiah 2, 11, and 66.

One may be in general agreement with our writings up to this point but not agree with the view of a literal millennial age (the Pre-Millennial view). However, God's redemption is a process that works its way out in stages. It makes sense to me that there would be an age in which the human race would work out their salvation according to all of the promises of sanctified living. These promises lie outside our potential until Satan is bound. This will forever prove the promises of God. It will show that what God promised was truly attainable by faith and obedience. After this era will come a New Jerusalem, New Heavens and a New Earth (Revelation 21, 22).

During the Millennial Age, "the meek will inherit the earth" (Ps. 37:11; Matt. 5: 5) and Israel will receive its full inheritance of land according to the Scriptures. The whole earth will be a land of promise. The Scriptures indicate that the nations will take part in practices that until that time were only enjoined on the Jews (the Sabbath, New Moon and Tabernacles, Isa. 66:23; Zech. 14:16). We do not know the extent to which Jewish biblical practice will become universal. According to the prophets, the Jewish people will still live out a pictorial representation of truth for the sake of the nations.

In that day, the Jewish nation will be a global teaching center and all nations will come up to Jerusalem (Isaiah 2: 2–3). Whether the Temple and its sacrifices have been literally or symbolically restored, the full meaning of the atonement of Yeshua will be taught there. Israel's irrevocable gifts and call will be fully realized in the glorious fulfillment envisioned by the ancient prophets who saw her as the chief of the nations. Israel will bestow prosperity on the nations and the nations will bring her their wealth. Isaiah 27:16 says that, "Israel will blossom and bud and fill the whole earth with fruit." She will serve the Lord as a kingdom of priests alongside the resurrected and translated Bride Queen, the Church. What great celebrations will take place, bringing together all the nations of the earth under God!

Every nation has a unique glory that cannot be replaced by any other. So in Revelation 21 and 22 we read the description beyond the Millennium of a New Jerusalem in the age of New Heavens and a New Earth. We will see the everlasting Jewish identification of the Holy City, for the names of the twelve tribes of Israel are over its gates and the names of the twelve Jewish Apostles adorn its foundation stones. All of the nations stream into it bringing their riches. Does this only mean material riches? Of course not, it means the unique glorious contributions of culture that each nation will contribute to the New Jerusalem. I imagine wonderful multi-cultural artistic celebrations of astonishing beauty.

Many have the idea that the goal of redemption is the elimination of distinct peoples, but this is not true. There is a unique redemptive purpose and contribution from each nation. No individual is just like any other, nor is any nation like another. Indeed, we see in today's multicultural movement a satanically perverse distortion of this truth, declaring that all cultures are created equal and that there are no standards by which to judge cultures (cultural relativism). On the contrary, when the demonic aspects of cultures are cast out and the elements of God's grace are redeemed, there will be an astounding biblical multiculturalism that enriches us all. The beauty and diversity of this life will never allow us to be bored. We will experience the glory of God, the glory of the Bride, the glory of Israel and the glory of all the nations intertwined in the New Jerusalem.

In order to better understand these biblical themes, readers are encouraged to study the following passages: Isaiah 60:1–12, Isaiah 11, Isaiah 2, Isaiah 49:6, Isaiah 27:6, Jeremiah 33, Jeremiah 31, and Revelation 20, 21.

If you agree with the vision that's been shared here, you're one of a growing number of Jewish and Gentile believers who are looking for new ways to work together and take action. We desire to see the Messianic movement well established in every major Jewish population center in the world. In addition, we are actively sharing with those in the Church to urge them to pray for Israel's salvation, to understand the importance of the Messianic congregational movement both locally and in Israel, and to catch a vision for seeing Messianic Jews restored to their proper place in the Body of the Messiah. Finally, we encourage each local church to become a house of witness, show deeds of love and kindness, and financially invest in a Messianic vision, supporting the growth of newly planted congregations, young leaders and other Messianic works as God leads.

The work of reconciliation between representatives of the Church and Messianic Jewish leaders presses forward. These efforts do not need media stars but true builders in the Church. We are looking for those who believe in prayerful reconciliation, and the representative repentance and forgiveness described by John Dawson. We believe that there will be many more gatherings of leaders representing Israel and the Church repenting and forgiving one another. Meetings will begin with addressing the wounds caused by the Church's rejection of the legitimate Jewish followers of Yeshua, beginning with the councils of the second-century Church and continuing into the Patristic Age. These gatherings will provoke much prayer, lots of tears and a generous application of the blood of the Lamb to centuries of accumulated sin. The Church will repent of the statement, "He who would be both Christian and Jew can be neither Christian nor Jew." Messianic Jews will repent for the history of their people who failed to embrace Yeshua as Messiah and Lord.

This must include a broad representation of several nations and the different historic streams in the Church. The Spirit has been stirring important men to come together for this end. We need you to pray for us as we seek official Church decisions as part of the Toward Jerusalem Council II project. We urge our counterparts to embrace the Messianic Jewish community, affirm its calling to live a Jewish life and remain part of Israel.

Let us pray together for these ends, the restoration of the Church, the restoration of Israel, and the saved remnant of Israel. As the Church actively fulfills her call and destiny, she is helping to restore Israel's irrevocable call, which is key to world redemption.

BIBLIOGRAPHY

Bockmuehl, Markus. *Jewish Law in Gentile Churches: Halakah and the Beginning of Christian Public Ethics.* Edinburgh: T. & T. Clark Publishers, 2000.

Butler, Joseph. *Butler's Analogy of Religion, Natural and Revealed, to the Constitution and Course of Nature.* Ed. William E. Gladstone. London: Oxford University Press, 1895.

Dawson, John. *Healing America's Wounds.* Ventura, CA: Regal Books, Division of Gospel Light, 1994.

Hocken, Peter. *The Glory and the Shame: Reflections on the 20th Century Outpouring of the Holy Spirit.* Guildford, Surrey, U.K.: Eagle Publications, 1994.

Kasdan, Barney. *God's Appointed Times: A Practical Guide for Understanding and Celebrating the Biblical Holidays.* Clarksville, Md: Messianic Jewish Publishers, 1993.

Kline, Meredith G. *Images of the Spirit.* Grand Rapids: Baker Book House, 1980.

McComiskey, Thomas E. The Covenants of Promise: *A Theology of the Old Testament Covenants.* Grand Rapids: Baker Book House, 1985.

Peters, Joan. *From Time Immemorial: The Origins of the Arab-Jewish Conflict Over Palestine.* New York: Harper and Row, 1984.

Schoenfeld, Hugh. *A History of Jewish Christianity from the First to the Twentieth Century.* London: Duckworth Publishers, 1936.

OTHER RELATED RESOURCES

Complete Jewish Bible: *A New English Version*

—Dr. David H. Stern

Presenting the Word of God as a unified Jewish book, the *Complete Jewish Bible* is a new version for Jews and non-Jews alike. It connects Jews with the Jewishness of the Messiah, and non-Jews with their Jewish roots. Names and key terms are returned to their original Hebrew and presented in easy-to-understand transliterations, enabling the reader to say them the way Yeshua (Jesus) did! 1697 pages.

Hardback	978-9653590151	**JB12**	$34.99
Paperback	978-9653590182	**JB13**	$29.99
Leather Cover	978-9653590199	**JB15**	$59.99
Large Print (12 Pt font)	978-1880226483	**JB16**	$49.99

Also available in French and Portuguese.

Jewish New Testament

—Dr. David H. Stern

The New Testament is a Jewish book, written by Jews, initially for Jews. Its central figure was a Jew. His followers were all Jews; yet no other version really communicates its original, essential Jewishness. Uses neutral terms and Hebrew names. Highlights Jewish references and corrects mistranslations. Freshly translated into English from Greek, this is a must read to learn about first-century faith. 436 pages

Hardback	978-9653590069	**JB02**	$19.99
Paperback	978-9653590038	**JB01**	$14.99
Spanish	978-1936716272	**JB17**	$24.99

Also available in French, German, Polish, Portuguese and Russian.

Jewish New Testament Commentary

—Dr. David H. Stern

This companion to the *Jewish New Testament* enhances Bible study. Passages and expressions are explained in their original cultural context. 15 years of research. 960 pages.

Hardback	978-9653590083	**JB06**	$34.99
Paperback	978-9653590113	**JB10**	$29.99

Psalms & Proverbs *Tehillim* תְּהִלִּים-*Mishlei* מִשְׁלֵי

—Translated by Dr. David Stern

Contemplate the power in these words anytime, anywhere: Psalms-*Tehillim* offers uplifting words of praise and gratitude, keeping us focused with the right attitude; Proverbs-*Mishlei* gives us the wisdom for daily living, renewing our minds by leading us to examine our actions, to discern good from evil, and to decide freely to do the good. Makes a wonderful and meaningful gift. Softcover, 224 pages.

978-1936716692	LB90	$9.99

Messianic Judaism *A Modern Movement With an Ancient Past*
—David H. Stern

An updated discussion of the history, ideology, theology and program for Messianic Judaism. A challenge to both Jews and non-Jews who honor Yeshua to catch the vision of Messianic Judaism. 312 pages

	978-1880226339	**LB62**	$17.99

Restoring the Jewishness of the Gospel
A Message for Christians
—David H. Stern

Introduces Christians to the Jewish roots of their faith, challenges some conventional ideas, and raises some neglected questions: How are both the Jews and "the Church" God's people? Is the Law of Moses in force today? Filled with insight! Endorsed by Dr. Darrell L. Bock. 110 pages

English	978-1880226667	**LB70**	$9.99
Spanish	978-9653590175	**JB14**	$9.99

Come and Worship *Ways to Worship from the Hebrew Scriptures*
—Compiled by Barbara D. Malda

We were created to worship. God has graciously given us many ways to express our praise to him. Each way fits a different situation or moment in life, yet all are intended to bring honor and glory to him. When we believe that he is who he says he is [see *His Names are Wonderful!*] and that his Word is true, worship flows naturally from our hearts to his. Softcover, 128 pages.

	978-1936716678	**LB88**	$9.99

His Names Are Wonderful
Getting to Know God Through His Hebrew Names
—Elizabeth L. Vander Meulen and Barbara D. Malda

In Hebrew thought, names did more than identify people; they revealed their nature. God's identity is expressed not in one name, but in many. This book will help readers know God better as they uncover the truths in his Hebrew names. 160 pages.

	978-1880226308	**LB58**	$9.99

The Return of the Kosher Pig *The Divine Messiah in Jewish Thought*
—Rabbi Tzahi Shapira

The subject of Messiah fills many pages of rabbinic writings. Hidden in those pages is a little known concept that the Messiah has the same authority given to God. Based on the Scriptures and traditional rabbinic writings, this book shows the deity of Yeshua from a new perspective. You will see that the rabbis of old expected the Messiah to be divine. Softcover, 352 pages.

"One of the most interesting and learned tomes I have ever read. Contained within its pages is much with which I agree, some with which I disagree, and much about which I never thought. Rabbi Shapria's remarkable book cannot be ignored."
—Dr. Paige Patterson, President, Southwest Baptist Theological Seminary

	978-1936716456	**LB81**	$ 39.99

Matthew Presents Yeshua, King Messiah *A Messianic Commentary*
—Rabbi Barney Kasdan

Few commentators are able to truly present Yeshua in his Jewish context. Most don't understand his background, his family, even his religion, and consequently really don't understand who he truly is. This commentator is well versed with first-century Jewish practices and thought, as well as the historical and cultural setting of the day, and the 'traditions of the Elders' that Yeshua so often spoke about. Get to know Yeshua, the King, through the writing of another rabbi, Barney Kasdan. 448 pages

978-1936716265   **LB76** $29.99

James the Just Presents Application of Torah
A Messianic Commentary
—Dr. David Friedman

James (Jacob) one of the Epistles written to first century Jewish followers of Yeshua. Dr. David Friedman, a former Professor of the Israel Bible Institute has shed new light for Christians from this very important letter.

978-1936716449   **LB82** $14.99

Jude On Faith and the Destructive Influence of Heresy
A Messianic Commentary
—Rabbi Joshua Brumbach

Almost no other canonical book has been as neglected and overlooked as the Epistle of Jude. This little book may be small, but it has a big message that is even more relevant today as when it was originally written.

978-1-936716-78-4   **LB97** $14.99

Conveying Our Heritage A Messianic Jewish Guide to Home Practice
—Daniel C. Juster, Th.D. Patricia A. Juster

Throughout history the heritage of faith has been conveyed within the family and the congregation. The first institution in the Bible is the family and only the family can raise children with an adequate appreciation of our faith and heritage. This guide exists to help families learn how to pass on the heritage of spiritual Messianic Jewish life. Softcover, 86 pages

978-1936716739   **LB93** $8.99

Mutual Blessing *Discovering the Ultimate Destiny of Creation*
—Daniel C. Juster

To truly love as God loves is to see the wonder and richness of the distinct differences in all of creation and his natural order of interdependence. This is the way to mutual blessing and the discovery of the ultimate destiny of creation. Learn how to become enriched and blessed as you enrich and bless others and all that is around you! Softcover, 135 pages

978-1936716746   **LB94** $9.99

At the Feet of Rabbi Gamaliel
Rabbinic Influence in Paul's Teachings
—David Friedman, Ph.D.

Paul (Shaul) was on the "fast track" to becoming a sage and Sanhedrin judge, describing himself as passionate for the Torah and the traditions of the fathers, typical for an aspiring Pharisee: "…trained at the feet of Gamaliel in every detail of the Torah of our forefathers. I was a zealot for God, as all of you are today" (Acts 22.3, CJB). Did Shaul's teachings reflect Rabbi Gamaliel's instructions? Did Paul continue to value the Torah and Pharisaic tradition? Did Paul create a 'New' Theology? The results of the research within these pages and its conclusion may surprise you. Softcover, 100 pages.

978-1936716753   **LB95** $8.99

Debranding God *Revealing His True Essence*
—Eduardo Stein

The process of 'debranding' God is to remove all the labels and fads that prompt us to understand him as a supplier and ourselves as the most demanding of customers. Changing our perception of God also changes our perception of ourselves. In knowing who we are in relationship to God, we discover his, and our, true essence. Softcover, 252 pages.

978-1936716708   **LB91** $16.99

Under the Fig Tree *Messianic Thought Through the Hebrew Calendar*
—Patrick Gabriel Lumbroso

Take a daily devotional journey into the Word of God through the Hebrew Calendar and the Biblical Feasts. Learn deeper meaning of the Scriptures through Hebraic thought. Beautifully written and a source for inspiration to draw closer to Adonai every day. Softcover, 407 pages.

978-1936716760   **LB96** $25.99

Under the Vine *Messianic Thought Through the Hebrew Calendar*
—Patrick Gabriel Lumbroso

Journey daily through the Hebrew Calendar and Biblical Feasts into the B'rit Hadashah (New Testament) Scriptures as they are put in their rightful context, bringing Judaism alive in it's full beauty. Messianic faith was the motor and what gave substance to Abraham's new beliefs, hope to Job, trust to Isaac, vision to Jacob, resilience to Joseph, courage to David, wisdom to Solomon, knowledge to Daniel, and divine Messianic authority to Yeshua. Softcover, 412 pages.

978-1936716654   **LB87** $25.99

The Revolt of Rabbi Morris Cohen

Exploring the Passion & Piety of a Modern-day Pharisee
—Anthony Cardinale

A brilliant school psychologist, Rabbi Morris Cohen went on a one-man strike to protest the systematic mislabeling of slow learning pupils as "Learning Disabled" (to extract special education money from the state). His disciplinary hearing, based on the transcript, is a hilarious read! This effusive, garrulous man with an irresistible sense of humor lost his job, but achieved a major historic victory causing the reform of the billion-dollar special education program. Enter into the mind of an eighth-generation Orthodox rabbi to see how he deals spiritually with the loss of everything, even the love of his children. This modern-day Pharisee discovered a trusted friend in the author (a born again believer in Jesus) with whom he could openly struggle over Rabbinic Judaism as well as the concept of Jesus (Yeshua) as Messiah. Softcover, 320 pages.

978-1936716722   **LB92** $19.99

Stories of Yeshua

—Jim Reimann, Illustrator Julia Filipone-Erez

Children's Bible Storybook with four stories about Yeshua (Jesus).
Yeshua is Born: The Bethlehem Story based on Lk 1:26-35 & 2:1-20; *Yeshua and Nicodemus in Jerusalem* based on Jn 3:1-16; *Yeshua Loves the Little Children of the World* based on Matthew 18:1–6 & 19:13–15; *Yeshua is Alive-The Empty Tomb in Jerusalem* based on Matthew 26:17-56, Jn 19:16-20:18, Lk 24:50-53. Ages 3-7, Softcover, 48 pages.

978-1936716685   **LB89** $14.99

To the Ends of the Earth – How the First Jewish Followers of Yeshua Transformed the Ancient World

— Dr. Jeffrey Seif

Everyone knows that the first followers of Yeshua were Jews, and that Christianity was very Jewish for the first 50 to 100 years. It's a known fact that there were many congregations made up mostly of Jews, although the false perception today is, that in the second century they disappeared. Dr. Seif reveals the truth of what happened to them and how these early Messianic Jews influenced and transformed the behavior of the known world at that time.

978-1936716463   **LB83** $17.99

Passion for Israel: *A Short History of the Evangelical Church's Support of Israel and the Jewish People*

—Dan Juster

History reveals a special commitment of Christians to the Jews as God's still elect people, but the terrible atrocities committed against the Jews by so-called Christians have overshadowed the many good deeds that have been performed. This important history needs to be told to help heal the wounds and to inspire more Christians to stand together in support of Israel.

978-1936716401   **LB78** $9.99

Jewish Roots and Foundations of the Scriptures I
—John Fischer, Th.D, Ph.D.

An outstanding evangelical leader once said: "There is something shallow about a Christianity that has lost its Jewish roots." A beautiful painting is a careful interweaving of a number of elements. Among other things, there are the background, the foreground and the subject. Discovering the roots of your faith is a little like appreciating the various parts of a painting. In the background is the panorama of preparation and pictures found in the Old Testament. In the foreground is the landscape and light of the first century Jewish setting. All of this is intricately connected with and highlights the subject—which becomes the flowering of all these aspects—the coming of God to earth and what that means for us. Discovering and appreciating your roots in this way broadens, deepens and enriches your faith and your understanding of Scripture. This audio is 32 hours of live class instruction - audio is clear and easy to understand.

9781936716623   **LCD03** $49.99

The Gospels in their Jewish Context
—John Fischer, Th.D, Ph.D.

An examination of the Jewish background and nature of the Gospels in their contemporary political, cultural and historical settings, emphasizing each gospel's special literary presentation of Yeshua, and highlighting the cultural and religious contexts necessary for understanding each of the gospels. 32 hours of audio/video instruction on MP3-DVD and pdf of syllabus.

978-1936716241   **LCD01** $49.99

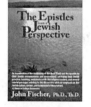

The Epistles from a Jewish Perspective
—John Fischer, Th.D, Ph.D.

An examination of the relationship of Rabbi Shaul (the Apostle Paul) and the Apostles to their Jewish contemporaries and environment; surveys their Jewish practices, teaching, controversy with the religious leaders, and many critical passages, with emphasis on the Jewish nature, content, and background of these letters. 32 hours of audio/video instruction on MP3-DVD and pdf of syllabus.

978-1936716258   **LCD02** $49.99

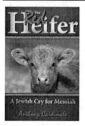

The Red Heifer *A Jewish Cry for Messiah*
—Anthony Cardinale

Award-winning journalist and playwright Anthony Cardinale has traveled extensively in Israel, and recounts here his interviews with Orthodox rabbis, secular Israelis, and Palestinian Arabs about the current search for a red heifer by Jewish radicals wishing to rebuild the Temple and bring the Messiah. These real-life interviews are interwoven within an engaging and dramatic fictional portrayal of the diverse people of Israel and how they would react should that red heifer be found. Readers will find themselves in the Land, where they can hear learned rabbis and ordinary Israelis talking about the red heifer and dealing with all the related issues and the imminent coming and identity of Messiah.

978-1936716470   LB79 $19.99

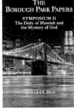

The Borough Park Papers
—Multiple Authors

As you read the New Testament, you "overhear" debates first-century Messianic Jews had about critical issues, e.g. Gentiles being "allowed" into the Messianic kingdom (Acts 15). Similarly, you're now invited to "listen in" as leading twenty-first century Messianic Jewish theologians discuss critical issues facing us today. Some ideas may not fit into your previously held pre-suppositions or pre-conceptions. Indeed, you may find some paradigm shifting in your thinking. We want to share the thoughts of these thinkers with you, our family in the Messiah.

Symposium I:
The Gospel and the Jewish People
248 pages

978-1936716593   LB84 $39.95

Symposium II:
The Deity of Messiah and the Mystery of God
211 pages

978-1936716609   LB85 $39.95

Symposium III:
How Jewish Should the Messianic Community Be?

978-1936716616   LB86 $39.95

On The Way to Emmaus: *Searching the Messianic Prophecies*
—Dr. Jacques Doukhan

An outstanding compilation of the most critical Messianic prophecies by a renowned conservative Christian Scholar, drawing on material from the Bible, Rabbinic sources, Dead Sea Scrolls, and more.

978-1936716432   LB80 $14.99

Yeshua *A Guide to the Real Jesus and the Original Church*
—Dr. Ron Moseley

Opens up the history of the Jewish roots of the Christian faith. Illuminates the Jewish background of Yeshua and the Church and never flinches from showing "Jesus was a Jew, who was born, lived, and died, within first century Judaism." Explains idioms in the New Testament. Endorsed by Dr. Brad Young and Dr. Marvin Wilson. 213 pages.

978-1880226681   **LB29** $12.99

Gateways to Torah *Joining the Ancient Conversation on the Weekly Portion*
—Rabbi Russell Resnik

From before the days of Messiah until today, Jewish people have read from and discussed a prescribed portion of the Pentateuch each week. Now, a Messianic Jewish Rabbi, Russell Resnik, brings another perspective on the Torah, that of a Messianic Jew. 246 pages.

978-1880226889   **LB42** $15.99

Creation to Completion *A Guide to Life's Journey from the Five Books of Moses*
—Rabbi Russell Resnik

Endorsed by Coach Bill McCartney, Founder of Promise Keepers & Road to Jerusalem: "Paul urged Timothy to study the Scriptures (2 Tim. 3:16), advising him to apply its teachings to all aspects of his life. Since there was no New Testament then, this rabbi/apostle was convinced that his disciple would profit from studying the Torah, the Five Books of Moses, and the Old Testament. Now, Rabbi Resnik has written a warm devotional commentary that will help you understand and apply the Law of Moses to your life in a practical way." 256 pages

978-1880226322   **LB61** $14.99

Walk Genesis! Walk Exodus! Walk Leviticus! Walk Numbers! Walk Deuteronomy!
Messianic Jewish Devotional Commentaries
—Jeffrey Enoch Feinberg, Ph.D.

Using the weekly synagogue readings, Dr. Jeffrey Feinberg has put together some very valuable material in his "Walk" series. Each section includes a short Hebrew lesson (for the non-Hebrew speaker), key concepts, an excellent overview of the portion, and some practical applications. Can be used as a daily devotional as well as a Bible study tool.

Walk Genesis!	238 pages	978-1880226759	**LB34**	$12.99
Walk Exodus!	224 pages	978-1880226872	**LB40**	$12.99
Walk Leviticus!	208 pages	978-1880226926	**LB45**	$12.99
Walk Numbers!	211 pages	978-1880226995	**LB48**	$12.99
Walk Deuteronomy!	231 pages	978-1880226186	**LB51**	$12.99
SPECIAL! Five-book Walk!		5 Book Set **Save $10**	**LK28**	$54.99

Good News According To Matthew
—Dr. Henry Einspruch

English translation with quotations from the Tanakh (Old Testament) capitalized and printed in Hebrew. Helpful notations are included. Lovely black and white illustrations throughout the book. 86 pages.

978-1880226025	**LB03**	$4.99
Also available in Yiddish.	**LB02**	$4.99

They Loved the Torah *What Yeshua's First Followers Really Thought About the Law*
—Dr. David Friedman

Although many Jews believe that Paul taught against the Law, this book disproves that notion. An excellent case for his premise that all the first followers of the Messiah were not only Torah-observant, but also desired to spread their love for God's entire Word to the gentiles to whom they preached. 144 pages. Endorsed by Dr. David Stern, Ariel Berkowitz, Rabbi Dr. Stuart Dauermann & Dr. John Fischer.

978-1880226940   **LB47** $9.99

The Distortion *2000 Years of Misrepresenting the Relationship Between Jesus the Messiah and the Jewish People*
—Dr. John Fischer & Dr. Patrice Fischer

Did the Jews kill Jesus? Did they really reject him? With the rise of global anti–Semitism, it is important to understand what the Gospels teach about the relationship between Jewish people and their Messiah. 2000 years of distortion have made this difficult. Learn how the distortion began and continues to this day and what you can do to change it. 126 pages. Endorsed by Dr. Ruth Fleischer, Rabbi Russell Resnik, Dr. Daniel C. Juster, Dr. Michael Rydelnik.

978-1880226254   **LB54** $11.99

God's Appointed Times *A Practical Guide to Understanding and Celebrating the Biblical Holidays* – **New Edition.**

—Rabbi Barney Kasdan

The Biblical Holy Days teach us about the nature of God and his plan for mankind, and can be a source of God's blessing for all believers–Jews and Gentiles–today. Includes historical background, traditional Jewish observance, New Testament relevance, and prophetic significance, plus music, crafts and holiday recipes. 145 pages.

English	978-1880226353	**LB63**	$12.99
Spanish	978-1880226391	**LB59**	$12.99

God's Appointed Customs *A Messianic Jewish Guide to the Biblical Lifecycle and Lifestyle*

— Rabbi Barney Kasdan

Explains how biblical customs are often the missing key to unlocking the depths of Scripture. Discusses circumcision, the Jewish wedding, and many more customs mentioned in the New Testament. Companion to *God's Appointed Times*. 170 pages.

English	978-1880226636	**LB26**	$12.99
Spanish	978-1880226551	**LB60**	$12.99

Celebrations of the Bible *A Messianic Children's Curriculum*

Did you know that each Old Testament feast or festival finds its fulfillment in the New? They enrich the lives of people who experience and enjoy them. Our popular curriculum for children is in a brand new, user-friendly format. The lay-flat at binding allows you to easily reproduce handouts and worksheets. Celebrations of the Bible has been used by congregations, Sunday schools, ministries, homeschoolers, and individuals to teach children about the biblical festivals. Each of these holidays are presented for Preschool (2-K), Primary (Grades 1-3), Junior (Grades 4-6), and Children's Worship/Special Services. 208 pages.

978-1880226261	**LB55**	$24.99

Passover: *The Key That Unlocks the Book of Revelation*
—Daniel C. Juster, Th.D.

Is there any more enigmatic book of the Bible than Revelation? Controversy concerning its meaning has surrounded it back to the first century. Today, the arguments continue. Yet, Dan Juster has given us the key that unlocks the entire book—the events and circumstances of the Passover/Exodus. By interpreting Revelation through the lens of Exodus, Dan Juster provides a unified overview that helps us read Revelation as it was always meant to be read, as a drama of spiritual conflict, deliverance, and above all, worship. He also shows how this final drama, fulfilled in Messiah, resonates with the Torah and all of God's Word. — Russ Resnik, Executive Director, Union of Messianic Jewish Congregations.

978-1936716210	**LB74**	$10.99

The Messianic Passover Haggadah
Revised and Updated
—Rabbi Barry Rubin and Steffi Rubin.

Guides you through the traditional Passover seder dinner, step-by-step. Not only does this observance remind us of our rescue from Egyptian bondage, but, we remember Messiah's last supper, a Passover seder. The theme of redemption is seen throughout the evening. What's so unique about our Haggadah is the focus on Yeshua (Jesus) the Messiah and his teaching, especially on his last night in the upper room. 36 pages.

English	978-1880226292	**LB57**	$4.99
Spanish	978-1880226599	**LBSP01**	$4.99

The Messianic Passover Seder Preparation Guide
Includes recipes, blessings and songs. 19 pages.

English	978-1880226247	**LB10**	$2.99
Spanish	978-1880226728	**LBSP02**	$2.99

The Sabbath *Entering God's Rest*
—Barry Rubin & Steffi Rubin

Even if you've never celebrated Shabbat before, this book will guide you into the rest God has for all who would enter in—Jews and non-Jews. Contains prayers, music, recipes; in short, everything you need to enjoy the Sabbath, even how to observe havdalah, the closing ceremony of the Sabbath. Also discusses the Saturday or Sunday controversy. 48 pages.

978-1880226742   LB32 $6.99

Havdalah *The Ceremony that Completes the Sabbath*
—Dr. Neal & Jamie Lash

The Sabbath ends with this short, yet equally sweet ceremony called havdalah (separation). This ceremony reminds us to be a light and a sweet fragrance in this world of darkness as we carry the peace, rest, joy and love of the Sabbath into the work week. 28 pages.

978-1880226605   LB69 $4.99

Dedicate and Celebrate!
A Messianic Jewish Guide to Hanukkah
—Barry Rubin & Family

Hanukkah means "dedication" — a theme of significance for Jews and Christians. Discussing its historical background, its modern-day customs, deep meaning for all of God's people, this little book covers all the how-tos! Recipes, music, and prayers for lighting the menorah, all included! 32 pages.

978-1880226834   LB36 $4.99

The Conversation
An Intimate Journal of the Emmaus Encounter
—Judy Salisbury

"Then beginning with Moses and with all the prophets, He explained to them the things concerning Himself in all the Scriptures." Luke 24:27
If you've ever wondered what that conversation must have been like, this captivating book takes you there.

"The Conversation brings to life that famous encounter between the two disciples and our Lord Jesus on the road to Emmaus. While it is based in part on an imaginative reconstruction, it is filled with the throbbing pulse of the excitement of the sensational impact that our Lord's resurrection should have on all of our lives." ~ Dr. Walter Kaiser President Emeritus Gordon-Conwell Theological Seminary. Hardcover 120 pages.

Hardcover	978-1936716173	**LB73**	$14.99
Paperback	978-1936716364	**LB77**	$9.99

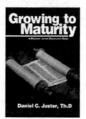

Growing to Maturity
A Messianic Jewish Discipleship Guide
—Daniel C. Juster, Th.D.

This discipleship series presents first steps of understanding and spiritual practice, tailored for the Jewish believer. It's purpose is to aid the believer in living according to Yeshua's will as a disciple, one who has learned the example of his teacher. The course is structured according to recent advances in individualized educational instruction. Discipleship is serious business and the material is geared for serious study and reflection. Each chapter is divided into short sections followed by study questions. 256 pages.

978-1936716227	**LB75**	$19.99

Growing to Maturity Primer: *A Messianic Jewish Discipleship Workbook*
—Daniel C. Juster, Th.D.

A basic book of material in question and answer form. Usable by everyone. 60 pages.

978-0961455507	**TB16**	$7.99

Proverbial Wisdom & Common Sense
—Derek Leman

A Messianic Jewish Approach to Today's Issues from the Proverbs Unique in style and scope, this commentary on the book of Proverbs, written in devotional style, is divided into chapters suitable for daily reading. A virtual encyclopedia of practical advice on family, sex, finances, gossip, honesty, love, humility, and discipline. Endorsed by Dr. John Walton, Dr. Jeffrey Feinberg and Rabbi Barney Kasdan. 248 pages.

978-1880226780	**LB35**	$14.99

That They May Be One *A Brief Review of Church Restoration Movements and Their Connection to the Jewish People*

—Daniel Juster, Th.D

Something prophetic and momentous is happening. The Church is finally fully grasping its relationship to Israel and the Jewish people. Author describes the restoration movements in Church history and how they connected to Israel and the Jewish people. Each one contributed in some way—some more, some less—toward the ultimate unity between Jews and Gentiles. Predicted in the Old Testament and fulfilled in the New, Juster believes this plan of God finds its full expression in Messianic Judaism. He may be right. See what you think as you read *That They May Be One*. 100 pages.

978-1880226711 **LB71** $9.99

The Greatest Commandment
How the Sh'ma Leads to More Love in Your Life

—Irene Lipson

"What is the greatest commandment?" Yeshua was asked. His reply—"Hear, O Israel, the Lord our God, the Lord is one, and you are to love Adonai your God with all your heart, with all your soul, with all your understanding, and all your strength." A superb book explaining each word so the meaning can be fully grasped and lived. Endorsed by Elliot Klayman, Susan Perlman, & Robert Stearns. 175 pages.

978-1880226360 **LB65** $12.99

Blessing the King of the Universe
Transforming Your Life Through the Practice of Biblical Praise

—Irene Lipson

Insights into the ancient biblical practice of blessing God are offered clearly and practically. With examples from Scripture and Jewish tradition, this book teaches the biblical formula used by men and women of the Bible, including the Messiah; points to new ways and reasons to praise the Lord; and explains more about the Jewish roots of the faith. Endorsed by Rabbi Barney Kasdan, Dr. Mitch Glaser, & Rabbi Dr. Dan Cohn-Sherbok. 144 pages.

978-1880226797 **LB53** $11.99

You Bring the Bagels, I'll Bring the Gospel
Sharing the Messiah with Your Jewish Neighbor
Revised Edition—Now with Study Questions

—Rabbi Barry Rubin

This "how-to-witness-to-Jewish-people" book is an orderly presentation of everything you need to share the Messiah with a Jewish friend. Includes Messianic prophecies, Jewish objections to believing, sensitivities in your witness, words to avoid. A "must read" for all who care about the Jewish people. Good for individual or group study. Used in Bible schools. Endorsed by Harold A. Sevener, Dr. Walter C. Kaiser, Dr. Erwin J. Kolb and Dr. Arthur F. Glasser. 253 pages.

| English | 978-1880226650 **LB13** | $12.99 |
| Te Tengo Buenas Noticias | 978-0829724103 **OBSP02** | $14.99 |

Making Eye Contact With God
A Weekly Devotional for Women
—Terri Gillespie

What kind of eyes do you have? Are they downcast and sad? Are they full of God's joy and passion? See yourself through the eyes of God. Using real life anecdotes, combined with scripture, the author reveals God's heart for women everywhere, as she softly speaks of the ways in which women see God. Endorsed by prominent authors: Dr. Angela Hunt, Wanda Dyson and Kathryn Mackel. 247 pages, hardcover.

978-1880226513   **LB68** $19.99

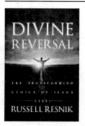

Divine Reversal
The Transforming Ethics of Jesus
—Rabbi Russell Resnik

In the Old Testament, God often reversed the plans of man. Yeshua's ethics continue this theme. Following his path transforms one's life from within, revealing the source of true happiness, forgiveness, reconciliation, fidelity and love. From the introduction, "As a Jewish teacher, Jesus doesn't separate matters of theology from practice. His teaching is consistently practical, ethical, and applicable to real life, even two thousand years after it was originally given." Endorsed by Jonathan Bernis, Dr. Daniel C. Juster, Dr. Jeffrey L. Seif, and Dr Darrell Bock. 206 pages

978-1880226803   **LB72** $12.99

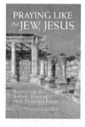

Praying Like the Jew, Jesus
Recovering the Ancient Roots of New Testament Prayer
—Dr. Timothy P. Jones

This eye-opening book reveals the Jewish background of many of Yeshua's prayers. Historical vignettes "transport" you to the times of Yeshua so you can grasp the full meaning of Messiah's prayers. Unique devotional thoughts and meditations, presented in down-to-earth language, provide inspiration for a more meaningful prayer life and help you draw closer to God. Endorsed by Mark Galli, James W. Goll, Rev. Robert Stearns, James F. Strange, and Dr. John Fischer. 144 pages.

978-1880226285   **LB56** $9.99

Growing Your Olive Tree Marriage *A Guide for Couples from Two Traditions*
—David J. Rudolph

One partner is Jewish; the other is Christian. Do they celebrate Hanukkah, Christmas or both? Do they worship in a church or a synagogue? How will the children be raised? This is the first book from a biblical perspective that addresses the concerns of intermarried couples, offering a godly solution. Includes highlights of interviews with intermarried couples. Endorsed by Walter C. Kaiser, Jr., Rabbi Dan Cohn-Sherbok, Jonathan Settel, Dr. Mitchell Glaser & Natalie Sirota. 224 pages.

978-1880226179   **LB50** $12.99

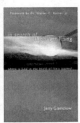

In Search of the Silver Lining *Where is God in the Midst of Life's Storms?*
—Jerry Gramckow

When faced with suffering, what are your choices? Storms have always raged. And people have either perished in their wake or risen above the tempests, shaping history by their responses...new storms are on the horizon. How will we deal with them? How will we shape history or those who follow us? The answer lies in how we view God in the midst of the storms. Endorsed by Joseph C. Aldrich, Ray Beeson, Dr. Daniel Juster. 176 pages.

978-1880226865   LB39 $10.99

The Voice of the Lord *Messianic Jewish Daily Devotional*
—Edited by David J. Rudolph

Brings insight into the Jewish Scriptures—both Old and New Testaments. Twenty-two prominent Messianic contributors provide practical ways to apply biblical truth. Start your day with this unique resource. Explanatory notes. Perfect companion to the Complete Jewish Bible (see page 2). Endorsed by Edith Schaeffer, Dr. Arthur F. Glaser, Dr. Michael L. Brown, Mitch Glaser and Moishe Rosen. 416 pages.

9781880226704   LB31 $19.99

Kingdom Relationships *God's Laws for the Community of Faith*
—Dr. Ron Moseley

Dr. Ron Moseley's Yeshua: A Guide to the Real Jesus and the Original Church has taught thousands of people about the Jewishness of not only Yeshua, but of the first followers of the Messiah.

In this work, Moseley focuses on the teaching of Torah -- the Five Books of Moses -- tapping into truths that greatly help modern-day members of the community of faith.

The first section explains the relationship of both the Jewish people and Christians to the Kingdom of God. The second section lists the laws that are applicable to a non-Jew living in the twenty-first century and outside of the land of Israel.

This book is needed because these little known laws of God's Kingdom were, according to Yeshua, the most salient features of the first-century community of believers. Yeshua even warned that anyone breaking these laws would be least in the Kingdom (Matt. 5:19). Additionally, these laws will be the basis for judgment at the end of every believer's life. 64 pages.

978-1880226841   LB37 $8.99

Train Up A Child *Successful Parenting For The Next Generation*
—Dr. Daniel L. Switzer

The author, former principal of Ets Chaiyim Messianic Jewish Day School, and father of four, combines solid biblical teaching with Jewish sources on child raising, focusing on the biblical holy days, giving fresh insight into fulfilling the role of parent. 188 pages. Endorsed by Dr. David J. Rudolph, Paul Lieberman, and Dr. David H. Stern.

978-1880226377   LB64 $12.99

Fire on the Mountain - *Past Renewals, Present Revivals and the Coming Return of Israel*
—Dr. Louis Goldberg

The term "revival" is often used to describe a person or congregation turning to God. Is this something that "just happens," or can it be brought about? Dr. Louis Goldberg, author and former professor of Hebrew and Jewish Studies at Moody Bible Institute, examines real revivals that took place in Bible times and applies them to today. 268 pages.

978-1880226858   **LB38** $15.99

Voices of Messianic Judaism *Confronting Critical Issues Facing a Maturing Movement*
—General Editor Rabbi Dan Cohn-Sherbok

Many of the best minds of the Messianic Jewish movement contributed their thoughts to this collection of 29 substantive articles. Challenging questions are debated: The involvement of Gentiles in Messianic Judaism? How should outreach be accomplished? Liturgy or not? Intermarriage? 256 pages.

978-1880226933   **LB46** $15.99

The Enduring Paradox *Exploratory Essays in Messianic Judaism*
—General Editor Dr. John Fischer

Yeshua and his Jewish followers began a new movement—Messianic Judaism—2,000 years ago. In the 20th century, it was reborn. Now, at the beginning of the 21st century, it is maturing. Twelve essays from top contributors to the theology of this vital movement of God, including: Dr. Walter C. Kaiser, Dr. David H. Stern, and Dr. John Fischer. 196 pages.

978-1880226902   **LB43** $13.99

The World To Come *A Portal to Heaven on Earth*
—Derek Leman

An insightful book, exposing fallacies and false teachings surrounding this extremely important subject... paints a hopeful picture of the future and dispels many non-biblical notions. Intriguing chapters: Magic and Desire, The Vision of the Prophets, Hints of Heaven, Horrors of Hell, The Drama of the Coming Ages. Offers a fresh, but old, perspective on the world to come, as it interacts with the prophets of Israel and the Bible. 110 pages.

978-1880226049   **LB67**   .$9.99

Hebrews Through a Hebrew's Eyes
—Dr. Stuart Sacks

Written to first-century Messianic Jews, this epistle, understood through Jewish eyes, edifies and encourages all. 119 pages. Endorsed by Dr. R.C. Sproul and James M. Boice.

978-1880226612   **LB23** $10.99

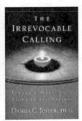

The Irrevocable Calling *Israel's Role As A Light To The Nations*
—Daniel C. Juster, Th.D.

Referring to the chosen-ness of the Jewish people, Paul, the Apostle, wrote "For God's free gifts and his calling are irrevocable" (Rom. 11:29). This messenger to the Gentiles understood the unique calling of his people, Israel. So does Dr. Daniel Juster, President of Tikkun Ministries Int'l. In *The Irrevocable Calling*, he expands Paul's words, showing how Israel was uniquely chosen to bless the world and how these blessings can be enjoyed today. Endorsed by Dr. Jack Hayford, Mike Bickle and Don Finto. 64 pages.

978-1880226346   **LB66** $8.99

Are There Two Ways of Atonement?
—Dr. Louis Goldberg

Here Dr. Louis Goldberg, long-time professor of Jewish Studies at Moody Bible Institute, exposes the dangerous doctrine of Two-Covenant Theology. 32 pages.

978-1880226056   **LB12** $ 4.99

Awakening *Articles and Stories About Jews and Yeshua*
—Arranged by Anna Portnov

Articles, testimonies, and stories about Jewish people and their relationship with God, Israel, and the Messiah. Includes the effective tract, "The Most Famous Jew of All." One of our best anthologies for witnessing to Jewish people. Let this book witness for you! Russian version also available. 110 pages.

English	978-1880226094	**LB15**	$ 6.99
Russian	978-1880226018	**LB14**	$ 6.99

The Unpromised Land *The Struggle of Messianic Jews Gary and Shirley Beresford*
—Linda Alexander

They felt God calling them to live in Israel, the Promised Land. Wanting nothing more than to live quietly and grow old together in the country of refuge for all Jewish people, little did they suspect what events would follow to try their faith. The fight to make *aliyah*, to claim their rightful inheritance in the Promised Land, became a battle waged not only for themselves, but also for Messianic Jews all over the world that wish to return to the Jewish homeland. Here is the true saga of the Beresford's journey to the land of their forefathers. 216 pages.

978-1880226568   **LB19** $ 9.99

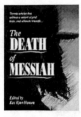

Death of Messiah *Twenty fascinating articles that address a subject of grief, hope, and ultimate triumph.*
—Edited by Kai Kjaer-Hansen

This compilation, written by well-known Jewish believers, addresses the issue of Messiah and offers proof that Yeshua—the true Messiah—not only died, but also was resurrected! 160 pages.

978-1880226582   **LB20** $ 8.99

Beloved Dissident *(A Novel)*
—Laurel West

A gripping story of human relationships, passionate love, faith, and spiritual testing. Set in the world of high finance, intrigue, and international terrorism, the lives of David, Jonathan, and Leah intermingle on many levels--especially their relationships with one another and with God. As the two men tangle with each other in a rising whirlwind of excitement and danger, each hopes to win the fight for Leah's love. One of these rivals will move Leah to a level of commitment and love she has never imagined--or dared to dream. Whom will she choose? 256 pages.

978-1880226766   **LB33** $ 9.99

Sudden Terror
—Dr. David Friedman

Exposes the hidden agenda of militant Islam. The author, a former member of the Israel Defense Forces, provides eye-opening information needed in today's dangerous world.

Dr. David Friedman recounts his experiences confronting terrorism; analyzes the biblical roots of the conflict between Israel and Islam; provides an overview of early Islam; demonstrates how the United States and Israel are bound together by a common enemy; and shows how to cope with terrorism and conquer fear. The culmination of many years of research and personal experiences. This expose will prepare you for what's to come! 160 pages.

978-1880226155   **LB49** $ 9.99

It is Good! *Growing Up in a Messianic Family*
—Steffi Rubin

Growing up in a Messianic Jewish family. Meet Tovah! Tovah (Hebrew for "Good") is growing up in a Messianic Jewish home, learning the meaning of God's special days. Ideal for young children, it teaches the biblical holidays and celebrates faith in Yeshua. 32 pages to read & color.

978-1880226063   **LB11** $ 4.99